virtuousreality

becoming the ideal woman

Vicki Courtney

LifeWay Christian Resources
Nashville, Tennessee

Produced by:
Student Ministry Publishing
LifeWay Christian Resources
One LifeWay Plaza
Nashville, TN 37234-0174
Customer Service: 1-800-458-2772

Editor: Art Herron
Production Specialist: Leanne Lawrence
Art Director: Jon Rodda

Dewey Decimal Classification: 248.834
Subject Heading: Christian Life / Single Women - College Students

ISBN 0-6330-0455-3

contents

about the writer 4

the crossseekers covenant 5

foreword 6

session one
the world's ideal woman – a virtual reality . .10

session two
the proverbs 31 woman – a virtuous reality . .22

session three
virtuous = a woman of worth 34

session four
virtuous = a woman of wisdom 46

session five
virtuous = a woman of purpose 60

session six
virtuous dating 76

leader's guide 92

crossseekers resources 95

virtuousreality
becoming the ideal woman

about the writer

about the writer

Vicki Courtney is the founder of CrossRoad Women's Ministry, a ministry devoted to meeting the spiritual needs of college women. She is the director of CrossRoad conferences and a speaker to college, singles, and women's groups. Her passion is to encourage college women to be in pursuit of the abundant life Christ refers to in John 10:10.

Vicki graduated from the University of Texas at Austin with a BA in Economics. She became a Christian during her junior year, while attending a conference for college students.

She resides in Austin, Texas with her husband, Keith, and their three children, Ryan, Paige and Hayden.

vicki courtney

The CrossSeekers® Covenant

"You will seek me and find me when you seek me with all your heart." Jeremiah 29:13

As a seeker of the cross of Christ, I am called to break away from trite, nonchalant, laissez-faire Christian living. I accept the challenge to divine daring, to consecrated recklessness for Christ, to devout adventure in the face of ridiculing contemporaries. Created in the image of God and committed to excellence as a disciple of Jesus Christ,

I will be a person of integrity

"Do your best to present yourself to God as one approved, a workman who does not need to be ashamed and who correctly handles the word of truth." 2 Timothy 2:15

My attitudes and actions reveal my commitment to live the kind of life Christ modeled for me—to speak the truth in love, to stand firm in my convictions, to be honest and trustworthy.

I will pursue consistent spiritual growth

"So then, just as you received Christ Jesus as Lord, continue to live in him, rooted and built up in him, strengthened in the faith as you were taught, and overflowing with thankfulness." Colossians 2:6-7

The Christian life is a continuing journey, and I am committed to a consistent, personal relationship with Jesus Christ, to faithful study of His Word, and to regular corporate spiritual growth through the ministry of the New Testament church.

I will speak and live a relevant, authentic, and consistent witness

"Always be prepared to give an answer to everyone who asks you to give the reason for the hope that you have." 1 Peter 3:15

I will tell others the story of how Jesus changed my life, and I will seek to live a radically changed life each day. I will share the good news of Jesus Christ with courage and boldness.

I will seek opportunities to serve in Christ's name

"The Spirit of the Lord is on me, because he has anointed me to preach good news to the poor. He has sent me to proclaim freedom for the prisoners and recovery of sight for the blind, to release the oppressed, to proclaim the year of the Lord's favor." Luke 4:18-19

I believe that God desires to draw all people into a loving, redeeming relationship with Him. As His disciple, I will give myself to be His hands to reach others in ministry and missions.

I will honor my body as the temple of God, dedicated to a lifestyle of purity

"Do you not know that your body is a temple of the Holy Spirit, who is in you, whom you have received from God? You are not your own; you were bought at a price. Therefore honor God with your body."
1 Corinthians 6:19-20

Following the example of Christ, I will keep my body healthy and strong, avoiding temptations and destructive personal vices. I will honor the gift of life by keeping myself sexually pure and free from addictive drugs.

I will be godly in all things, Christlike in all relationships

"Therefore, as God's chosen people, holy and dearly loved, clothe yourselves with compassion, kindness, humility, gentleness and patience. Bear with each other and forgive whatever grievances you may have against one another. Forgive as the Lord forgave you. And over all these virtues put on love, which binds them all together in perfect unity." Colossians 3:12-14

In every relationship and in every situation, I will seek to live as Christ would. I will work to heal brokenness, to value each person as a child of God, to avoid petty quarrels and harsh words, to let go of bitterness and resentment that hinder genuine Christian love.

Foreword
By Beth Moore

Few things in our culture concern me more than the devastating impact our sophisticated society is having upon young women. From early elementary school, girls are inundated with magazine covers, billboards, newspaper ads and shopping center windows selling an unreal, computer-perfect rack of bones with perfect skin and shiny hair. Sadly, we're buying it by the millions of dollars.

Our society claims to be concerned about epidemic teenage pregnancy and sexually transmitted diseases, yet all the while young women are media-discipled to cultivate their sensuality above all else. The number of teenage girls turning to plastic surgery, liposuction, and self-starvation is rising at an alarming rate. Today's youthful female has never had more opportunity to be beautiful and desirable and yet she has never been less secure.

The pressure is on. The stakes are high. Virtue is out. Adventure is in. Let's not kid ourselves into thinking that the effects are short term. These young women will take innumerable insecurities and an eschewed identity straight into the workplace, marriage and motherhood.

It is up to us to tell the truth. God's Word is our only standard of truth. He fearfully and wonderfully created each one of us, and only His Word can equip us with true identity, one that brings a godly confidence, security, satisfaction, and genuine success.

Vicki Courtney has done a masterful job of guiding young women to discover their true identity in God's Word. He has gifted her with an approach that exudes authenticity and grabs your attention. Targeted to college women, *Virtuous Reality* injects truth during arguably the most important decision-making years of a young woman's life. I know what a difference Christ can make in an insecure college girl's life. That's exactly when I surrendered my life to ministry and it stuck!

I'm honored to help introduce Vicki Courtney and her tremendous work *Virtuous Reality* to you. Both have been appointed for this generation. You will quickly discover that this woman knows what's she's talking about from pure, personal experience. Vicki Courtney has done her homework. If you do yours, you're going to be transformed.

How to use this book

Virtuous Reality: Becoming the Ideal Woman is designed to be used either in large or small group sessions. Specifically, it is designed to be used with young women in college or in the work force between the ages of 18-26.

Each session is written in an interactive style. This means you will discover:
- Questions and space for answers to be written in
- True and False questions
- Multiple choice questions
- Sidebar comments
- Statements which require your thought

You will discover at the end of each chapter a section entitled, *Encourage Your Group: Actions for Group Study.* If you are working through this book at a conference or in a small covenant group, you will want to examine the questions in this section for discussion with the others in your group.

You will also find a section at the end of each session entitled, *Between You and God.* This section is intended to encourage you to continue building your relationship with God. Hopefully the instructions will provide you some guidance in this area.

Finally, throughout the book you will find CrossSeekers icons beside a block of text. When you find the icon, it will encourage you to examine your spiritual walk through a look at the CrossSeekers Covenant which you find located on page 5. CrossSeekers is a spiritual transformational discipleship movement taking place throughout the country on college campuses and in young adult groups in churches.

For more information about CrossSeekers and how it can strengthen your desire to be a godly woman, please contact us on the web at:

www.crossseekers.org

Virtuous Reality
Becoming the Ideal Woman

"Who can find a virtuous woman? for her price *is* far above rubies.

The heart of her husband doth safely trust in her, so that he shall have no need of spoil.

She will do him good and not evil all the days of her life.

She seeketh wool, and flax, and worketh willingly with her hands.

She is like the merchants' ships; she bringeth her food from afar.

She riseth also while it is yet night, and giveth meat to her household, and a portion to her maidens.

She considereth a field, and buyeth it: with the fruit of her hands she planteth a vineyard.

She girdeth her loins with strength, and strengtheneth her arms.

She perceiveth that her merchandise *is* good: her candle goeth not out by night.

She layeth her hands to the spindle, and her hands hold the distaff.

She stretcheth out her hand to the poor; yea, she reacheth forth her hands to the needy.

She is not afraid of the snow for her household: for all her household *are* clothed with scarlet.

She maketh herself coverings of tapestry; her clothing *is* silk and purple.

Her husband is known in the gates, when he sitteth among the elders of the land.

She maketh fine linen, and selleth *it*; and delivereth girdles unto the merchant.

Strength and honour *are* her clothing; and she shall rejoice in time to come.

She openeth her mouth with wisdom; and in her tongue *is* the law of kindness.

She looketh well to the ways of her household, and eateth not the bread of idleness.

Her children arise up, and call her blessed; her husband *also*, and he praiseth her.

Many daughters have done virtuously, but thou excellest them all.

Favour *is* deceitful, and beauty *is* vain: *but* a woman *that* feareth the LORD, she shall be praised.

Give her of the fruit of her hands; and let her own works praise her in the gates"

Proverbs 31:10-31 (KJV).

Preface

In my years of teaching and speaking, I must admit that I have purposely avoided teaching on the Proverbs 31 woman. Quite frankly, she is rather intimidating to me. If she really does exist, I'm not sure I would even desire to run in her same circle. If this passage is to be taken literally, the two of us would not have much in common. For example, when I need a button sewn on a garment, I take it to the dry cleaners. I'm not even sure what "flax" is, and I'm curious as to whether or not "bringing her food in from afar" would include picking up take-out from a local restaurant. The verse about having maidens is appealing. I could probably handle "buying a field," but would struggle with planting a vineyard when I can't even keep an ivy plant alive. Could "strengthening her arms" include joining a health club or carrying my children around? If I am unable to sew, can I hire someone else to "layeth hands to the spindle" and still get credit? Would "stretching out my hand to the poor" include participating in the can food drive at my children's school? If her children are "clothed in scarlet" and she in "silk and purple" does this give me permission to shop at the finest stores and charge it? When she "opens her mouth with wisdom and kindness," does it include times when her children are fighting, the toilets need cleaning, and she has PMS? Does "eateth not the bread of idleness" mean that I must give up my fifteen-minute power nap in the afternoon? Did her children and husband "arise up and call her blessed" every single day? How did she manage that? If "beauty is vain," does that mean I must give up my manicured nails and natural blonde highlights? Last of all, what exactly does it mean to "feareth the Lord"?

One truth stands out: We are to be in pursuit of becoming a "virtuous" woman. For college women, this pursuit must begin today. The CrossSeekers' Covenant encourages us to be committed to excellence as a disciple of Jesus Christ. We are further encouraged to "accept the challenge to divine daring, to consecrated recklessness for Christ, to devout adventure in the face of ridiculing contemporaries." There is no doubt that the virtuous woman as defined by God's  standards will be subjected to the ridicule of this world. The virtuous woman is a rare find in today's world and her worth far above rubies. I don't know about you, but the thought of being a "rare find" is rather appealing to me. I've never been one to follow the crowd anyway. How about you? Will you join me in the journey to unravel the mystery behind the virtuous woman? Our search will not return void.

the world's ideal woman—
a virtual reality

The World's Ideal Woman– A Virtual Reality

What's Your Legacy?

Imagine viewing your own funeral many years from now. You are sitting at the back, undetected, as those closest to you come up one by one to say a few words about your life. Your husband, children, grandchildren, pastor, a co-worker, and a neighbor come up to summarize in paragraphs what your life was all about. What will they say? Will you be remembered for your contributions in the work force? Will you be remembered for donating large sums of money to worthy causes? Will you be remembered as being a friend to the friendless? Will you be remembered for your tireless devotion to the local church?

Your entire life has pointed to this very moment, and before your eyes, your legacy begins to unfold. Qualities you possessed on earth are molded into stories and memories and handed down to future generations. Your entire existence is summed up with words describing who you were as a person, what you accomplished, and the legacy you left behind. You begin to weep as you realize that your life is but a speck on the time line of eternity. Do you weep with tears of joy or regret as this truth begins to sink in? Would you do things differently if given another chance?

Fortunately, it is not too late. As college women, it is time to think about the legacy you will someday leave behind. Who you are today will impact who you are tomorrow. Are you in pursuit of developing qualities that will someday mold a legacy you can be proud of? Or, will you climb this ladder called life only to discover when you get to the top that it was leaning against the wrong wall?

You will only get one shot at this life. This is not a dress rehearsal. Believe it or not, the legacy you leave behind can impact your family's lineage for generations to come. Many women have failed to take this responsibility seriously. In a pleasure-seeking world that stresses instant gratification, little thought is given to developing qualities that will impact our own future, much less future generations.

As women, God has given us in His Word a standard to strive for during our brief time on earth. The Proverbs 31 woman possessed inner qualities that transcend from generation to generation. She is described as virtuous and noble and her worth is far above rubies. She is considered the ideal wife and mother. A man who finds such a woman is blessed for she is a rare find. For years, women have been intimidated by this woman and her many qualities. Will someone be able to look back on my life and claim I was a virtuous woman, a woman of noble character? Few women will be honored with this title. Will you be one of them? The choice is yours.

You are who you've been becoming!

SPIRITUAL GROWTH

Re-read Proverbs 31:10-31.

Check each statement below that applies to what you are feeling after reading the passage:

[ ] Give me a break! Is this woman for real?

[ ] My mother fits this to a tee!

[ ] This woman is incredibly retro!

[ ] No problem! My mother has been training me to become this woman.

[ ] I'm exhausted just hearing about all she did.

[ ] I'm never reading that passage again.

[ ] Sounds like a challenge, and I like a good challenge.

[ ] If this is the "ideal woman," I better get started.

Examine the following verses again and describe in your own words what you think the verses mean in today's language:

"She selects wool and flax and works with eager hands" (v. 13).

"She is like the merchant ships, bringing her food from afar" (v. 14).

"She gets up while it is still dark; she provides food for her family and portions for her servant girls" (v. 15).

"She considers a field and buys it;" (v. 16a).

"...her lamp does not go out at night" (v. 18b).

"In her hand she holds the distaff and grasps the spindle with her fingers" (v. 19).

"...for all of them are clothed in scarlet" (v. 21b).

"...she is clothed in fine linen and purple" (v. 22b).

"Her husband is respected at the city gate," (v. 23a).

"She is clothed with strength and dignity; she can laugh at the days to come" (v. 25).

"...faithful instruction is on her tongue" (v. 26b).

"She watches over the affairs of her household and does not eat the bread of idleness" (v. 27).

"Her children arise and call her blessed; her husband also, and he praises her:" (v. 28).

"Charm is deceptive, and beauty is fleeting; but a woman who fears the LORD is to be praised" (v. 30).

"...let her works bring her praise at the city gate" (v. 31b).

Which verses were intimidating to you? Why? State two reasons:
  1.
  2.

In this study, we will seek to answer these questions:
  • Who is this woman? Does she really exist?
  • Is it important that women today understand the Proverbs 31 woman?

- Is it possible in today's world to be a Proverbs 31 woman, or is she an outdated fixture of the past?
- Is she considered the "ideal woman" and if so, should we attempt to emulate her qualities?
- If we are not exactly like her, is it still possible to be a virtuous woman?
- What is God's definition of the ideal woman?

The Proverbs 31 Woman: A Virtuous Reality

Let me begin by saying that I am **not** an authority on the Proverbs 31 woman. Many different teaching angles have been used when interpreting this Scripture. It is not my desire to dissect it and leave you with a checklist of skills to develop. I can only offer you my own personal experience in striving to become a virtuous woman in light of this Scripture in my life. I have a long way to go, so allow me to be a fellow sojourner in this discovery of the ideal woman in God's eyes.

My Story:

My mother is a very successful career woman who returned to college to earn her degree after my brother and I entered grade school. In her late 40's, she attended law school and earned a law degree. She is currently a practicing attorney specializing in employment law in San Antonio, Texas. She raised me to believe that I could accomplish anything if I put my mind to it. During my childhood years, the housework was a shared duty between my mother and father, and we went out to eat frequently. My mother was a model of confidence and determination, and I wanted to be just like her.

I was not aware of the Proverbs 31 woman until my junior year in college. It was during that time that I became a Christian. Prior to that, I was a self-professed agnostic with feministic ideals. You can imagine my shock when I first read the Proverbs 31 description of a virtuous woman after becoming a Christian. She was way out of my league! I did not know how to cook, clean, garden, sew, or look well to the ways of a household in general. As a new believer, I wanted desperately to please my Father in heaven (not to mention my future husband), but didn't know where to begin. There weren't exactly a lot of courses I could sign up for in college to aid me in my quest to become a virtuous woman.

To further complicate things, I went on to marry my husband Keith. With this marriage, I became the proud daughter-in-law of the perfect mother-in-law. As you have guessed, she is a full-time homemaker with more recipes than I have brain cells. My husband claims she would take requests in the morning for breakfast and whip up something different for each person in the family. Needless to say, his mother was in charge of housekeeping and they rarely went out to eat.

I am sure you have gathered by now that I was short on homemaking skills when we first married. I was hesitant to even register for household appliances during our engagement for fear I would have to learn how to use them. My mother-in-law had thoughtfully given me recipes for my husband's favorite meals, and I remember being relieved that his favorite dishes could be found at many restaurants. Desiring to be a homemaker to my new husband, I gave it my best shot. No sooner than I had finally learned to prepare a meal without the fire alarm going off, I discovered we were expecting our first child. Thirteen months after we were married I became a full-time wife and mother.

In my early years of being a wife and mother, I would cringe at the very mention of the Proverbs 31 woman, whether in a Bible study or a discussion with my friends. She was a reminder of everything I was not. Everyone seemed to emphasize her domestic skills related to cooking, cleaning, sewing, gardening and caring for her husband and children. The more I heard about her virtuosity, the less confident I felt as a Christian wife and mother. In my lack of understanding, my attitude began to sour and I wondered what women had done to deserve such a difficult lot in life.

The more I tried to emulate the domestic skills of the virtuous woman, the more I failed. My husband was more than understanding and rarely complained about wearing pink t-shirts and underwear. Early in our marriage, I even overheard the poor man asking his mother how to get the mildew smell out of towels. It was a major feat for me to get everything cooked and on the table at the same time. My favorite cookbook was one that only contained recipes requiring six ingredients or less. If I remembered to clip coupons, many times I got to the store only to discover I had left them behind at home.

Surely there had to be more to life than rejoicing with a friend over a new method to remove spit up stains from a bib. Now don't get me wrong here, I LOVE being a mother. When my children were babies I loved rocking them until they fell asleep in my arms. I loved getting on the floor and playing with them and making up silly songs that would make them laugh. However, it quickly became clear that being creative with the kids didn't get the toilets cleaned and the beds made. It never seemed to be enough, and I perceived that reaching Proverbs 31 status was based more on an ability to perform domestic chores than to make a baby laugh.

The more frustrated I became, the more I wondered what my life might have been like had I pursued a path that would have highlighted my talents more. Prior to becoming a Christian, I would have defined an ideal woman much differently. I was torn between the world's definition of an ideal woman and God's definition of a virtuous woman. Could I find fulfillment in doing it God's way?

What caused my ongoing struggle to accept wholeheartedly the Bible's definition of a virtuous woman? If I invested everything I had into becoming the "ideal woman" as defined by God, would that be a legacy I could

> **"In his heart a man plans his course, but the Lord determines his steps"** (Prov. 16:9).

be proud of? Would my grandkids sit around and talk about Grandma's mean meat loaf recipe and how her house was always neat as a pin? Or, could they say these things and much more? Would I always struggle to find contentment in my pursuit of becoming a virtuous woman? Was it possible that I was still indoctrinated by the world's definition of the ideal woman?

The Ideal Woman: Fantasy or Reality?

How might the world define the ideal woman? List a couple of ideas.

1.
2.

How do you define the ideal woman? (Be honest.) Jot down four essentials you think the ideal woman possesses.

-
-
-
-

During a Bible study, I asked a group of college men to share, in general, what they considered the ideal woman to be. Many of the college women in the group concurred with their answers, claiming they were more than aware of the opinions among college men.

The bottom line? Many men feel the ideal woman would possess beauty, brains, bucks, and a great body!

Rank from 1-6 how much each factor below contributes to molding the ideal woman as defined by the world:

____media   ____Barbie

____church   ____the education system

____*Sports Illustrated Swimsuit Edition*   ____women

Mark an *X* on each line below to indicate approximately where you would rank according to the world's standard.

Beauty:

(——————————————————————————————)

It's what's on the inside that counts, right?   Supermodels hate me, I'm so beautiful.

Brains:

(——————————————————————————————)

I wish I had some.   I can explain photosynthesis.

Body:

(——————————————————————————————)

Unfortunately, I do have one.   Every summer, I look forward to
swimsuit shopping.

Bucks:

(——————————————————————————————)

Aren't those male deer?   Bill Gates calls me to borrow money.

I think if we are all honest, we would have to admit that much of how we define the ideal woman starts when we are young. For many, exposure to the world's definition of the ideal woman begins at home. Some are told to look pretty, lose weight, make straight A's, and pursue an education that would lend itself to making a good living. Some are exposed to parents going at break-neck speed to prove themselves to the world, and they are taught to follow their parents' example in order to survive. Even if parents do their best to stress God's ideal, it's only a matter of time before children discover what qualities the world applauds.

> "Charm
> is deceptive,
> and beauty
> is fleeting...."
> (Prov. 31:30).

> But the LORD said to Samuel, "Do not consider his appearance or his height, for I have rejected him. The LORD does not look at the things man looks at. Man looks at the outward appearance, but the LORD looks at the heart"
> (1 Sam. 16:7).

The Perfect Woman

By the time we reach adulthood, we have a pretty good idea of what it takes to fit the world's standard of an ideal woman. An expanded description of a woman esteemed by the world might include: independent, self-reliant, self-sufficient, confident, productive, glamourous, savvy, beautiful, professional, intelligent, successful and slender. This woman knows what she wants and she goes after it. She looks out for number one and isn't afraid to be assertive. She can have a career and a family. She is superwoman. She does it all and she does it well. She is at soccer games with her laptop and PTA meetings with her cell phone. She always looks polished and never seems tired. The world is at her fingertips. What can't be done at home, she hires out. She takes off from work to drive on field trips or bring cupcakes to school on her child's birthday. She has spent enough quality time with her children that they share their innermost thoughts and dreams with her. They never complain if she lacks time for them because they are proud of who she is and that she utilizes her talents in a productive manner.

I can honestly tell you that in my life, I have never met a woman like this. Most women who attempt to meet the above requirements are in therapy and popping Prozac like it's candy.

How do you feel about the world's standard for measuring the ideal woman? Check all that apply!

    [ ] I am REALLY angry!

    [ ] No big deal. I personally like getting kudos from the world.

    [ ] I'm shocked. I never realized the world's standard is so shallow.

    [ ] I will think twice about going out with a guy who follows the world's standard.

    [ ] I'm not surprised. It's just the way things are in the world today.

Have you fallen prey to the world's standard of the ideal woman?

    [ ] Yes   [ ] Not Sure   [ ] No

The Truth Hurts

This might help you take a more introspective look at yourself. Circle
T(rue) or **F**(alse).

T F I worry more about fat grams than having a daily quiet time.

T F When considering a major, I look for one that will enable me to pursue a career.

T F I would not have a problem going out in public without makeup.

T F I enjoy receiving compliments on my appearance.

T F My first thought when I rise in the morning is, "Where is my Bible" not "What should I wear today?"

T F I would feel more self-worth working part-time for a law firm than a church nursery.

T F If I look at a Victoria's Secret® catalog, it throws me into a major depression.

T F If I were to go out with a guy, kindness and respect would go much further than good looks and a sports car.

T F A bad hair day can affect my whole mood.

T F I am more impressed when I see a woman playing at the park with her kids than when I see a woman negotiating a business deal on a cell phone while watching her kids play.

T F When I am going out with someone I really like, I think more about what he is like on the inside than on the outside.

T F I would rather someone say I was kindhearted than pretty.

T F You can't get any more ideal than Princess Diana.

T F I am able to look in a full-length mirror while wearing my swimsuit and say, "I am fearfully and wonderfully made."

Before we can accept God's definition of the ideal woman, we must be willing to question the world's definition. We must also be honest when it comes to identifying which definition has had the most impact on our lives, personally. You may have laughed when answering the survey above, but the truth is, it is a serious matter. Women who are molded by the world's definition of the ideal woman can experience devastating consequences if their worth is misdefined. We will address self-worth in a future session, but first it is necessary to dispel the myth of the ideal woman as perpetuated by the world.

INTEGRITY

Summarize the following verses into your own words:

"What good will it be for a man if he gains the whole world, yet forfeits his soul? Or what can a man give in exchange for his soul?" (Matt. 16:26).

"For the wisdom of this world is foolishness in God's sight" (1 Cor. 3:19a).

"Do not love the world or anything in the world. If anyone loves the world, the love of the Father is not in him" (1 John 2:15).

"For everything in the world—the cravings of sinful man, the lust of his eyes and the boasting of what he has and does—comes not from the Father but from the world" (1 John 2:16).

Encourage Your Group: Actions for Group Study

WITNESS

The support verse for the CrossSeeker Covenant point of **witness** is: "Always be prepared to give an answer to everyone who asks you to give the reason for the hope that you have" (1 Pet. 3:15).

1. How can we lovingly stand as a witness against the world's definition of the ideal woman?

2. Are you prepared to be that witness? Why or why not?

3. Go back and re-read my story. Can you relate to my struggle? Share your thoughts.

4. In your own words, describe your idea of the "ideal woman" and what she would be like today.

5. Look at the chart on page 16 again. Which three factors, in your opinion, contribute most to molding the world's definition of the ideal woman? What other factors, not listed, might contribute to the world's definition?

6. Look at the chart on page 19. How have you been influenced by the world?

7. Re-read the Bible verses on page 20. Which verse impacted you the most? Why?

Between You and God

1. Are you in the process today of becoming the person you want to be tomorrow? If not, how might you change that?

2. Search your heart. Do you even desire to become a virtuous woman?

3. On page 18 re-read the description of "The Perfect Woman." Have you ever aspired to be this woman?

4. Do you think it is possible to be this woman?

5. Pray about the possibility of sharing your answers with an older, godly woman to aid you in gaining a more proper perspective.

6. Do you want to be a "rare find?" Pray and ask God to prepare your heart to receive His truth as His definition begins to unfold in future sessions.

the proverbs 31 woman–
a virtuous reality

The Proverbs 31 Woman–
A Virtuous Reality

V
I
R
Trustworthy
U
E

Interestingly, Proverbs 31:10-31 was written as a poem in acrostic format, with each verse beginning with a successive letter of the Hebrew alphabet. Although this passage has served as a guide to women, it was intended for a male audience with the intention of extolling a virtuous woman, or also translated, a wife of noble character.

Many times, well-meaning Christians have taught the passage of the Proverbs 31 woman and focused more on her domestic qualities than her internal attributes. I recently plugged "Proverbs 31" into my internet search engine and was amazed at the number of references it pulled up. Many were home pages created by women containing recipes, gardening tips, sewing patterns, parenting advice, and much more. Some were very enjoyable to read, while others were somewhat disturbing. One, in particular, actually claimed that in order to be a virtuous woman of noble character you must: cook, clean, sew, garden, and be a full-time mother. Another made the point that you are out of the will of God if you wear pants, short hair, or choose a method to educate your children other than home-schooling. *In my case, one, two, three strikes I'm out!*

I am certainly not saying that there is anything inherently wrong with the above mentioned convictions. I do, however, believe it is stretching it to imply that *all women* must exercise these same convictions to become a virtuous woman.

The Proverbs 31 woman possessed many virtues, and one could easily become overwhelmed or intimidated when reading through her description. She most likely did not wake up one morning virtuous, having finally accomplished all of the qualities listed in the passage. There must be some order in this pursuit to becoming an ideal woman in the eyes of God. What sets the virtuous woman apart as a woman who, "excels them all?" To discover the first step in our quest to becoming a virtuous woman, there is no better place to start than the very beginning. Proverbs 31:10b states that the virtuous woman is "worth far more than rubies."

In the Book of Job, he says, "Coral and jasper are not worthy of mention; the price of wisdom is beyond rubies" (Job 28:18).

Wisdom cannot be bought, traded for, or compared to. "It is hidden from the eyes of every living thing, concealed even from the birds of the air. Destruction and Death say, 'Only a rumor of it has reached our ears'" (Job 28:21, 22).

Who understands the way to wisdom? Circle the correct answer below. (verse 23)

Your pastor   Your guidance counselor   God

God alone holds the key to obtaining wisdom. After making it clear that wisdom is inaccessible to man, He tells us where it can be found.

What does God say to man in Job 28:28?

So, if a virtuous woman is "worth far more than rubies" and therefore possesses wisdom, then the bottom line is: A virtuous woman will... (Circle one.)

...cook biscuits from scratch.

...sew her own clothes.

...fear the Lord.

While many of the domestic qualities of the Proverbs 31 woman are standard for her time period and culture, the quality of "fearing the Lord" remains steadfast throughout the Bible.

Psalm 111:10 tells us that, "The fear of the LORD is the beginning of wisdom." Before we can begin to understand the mystery of obtaining wisdom (session 4), we must first explore what it is to fear the Lord.

Describe in your own words what you think "fear of the Lord" means.

_____

The type of fear referred to in the Proverbs 31 passage is filial, which is based in love. New Unger's Bible Dictionary describes this fear as the type that:

- dreads God's displeasure
- desires His favor
- reveres His holiness
- submits cheerfully to His will
- is grateful for His benefits, sincerely worships Him
- conscientiously obeys His commandments

Fear and love must coexist in us in order that either emotion may be healthy and we may please and rightly serve God.

Read Acts 9:31 in the New Testament. As you read, fill in the blanks.

"Then the church throughout Judea, Galilee and Samaria enjoyed a time of peace. It was strengthened; and encouraged by the _____ _____, it grew in numbers, living in the fear of the Lord."

Fear of the Lord originates with God and is bestowed upon man through the power of the Holy Spirit. The first step to fearing the Lord is to know the Author of life. Proverbs 19:23 says, "The fear of the LORD leads to life: Then one rests content, untouched by trouble." In John 14:6, Jesus claims, "I am the way and the truth and the life. No one comes to the Father except through me." He further says in John 10:10b, "I am come that they might have life, and that they might have it more abundantly."(KJV)

An abundant life is as difficult to come by as it is to be a woman of noble character. Most people will forfeit the abundant life for "just a life." The same path to fearing the Lord will lead us to a life abundant, full of hope, joy, and contentment. Like the virtuous woman in Proverbs 31:25, we too can laugh at the days to come.

To know the Author of life, we must have come to a point in our lives where we have placed our faith in Jesus Christ and acknowledged Him as the only way to God through the forgiveness of our sins. This is no doubt, the most important decision we will ever make (or not make) in our lives. Belief in Jesus Christ is the bridge to knowing God.

> "...a woman who fears the LORD is to be praised" (Prov. 31:30).

Most people will forfeit the abundant life for "just a life."

Read John 14:6 again. The only way to establish a personal relationship with God the Father is by: (choose one)

[ ] feeding the poor

[ ] attending church

[ ] getting baptized as an infant

[ ] practicing random acts of kindness

[ ] reading through the Bible once a year

[ ] giving money to Christian causes

[ ] believing in His Son

[ ] being a really good person

[ ] having grandparents who pray for you

[ ] raising awareness for land mine victims

Briefly describe two things you remember about your first encounter with the Author of life.

1.

2.

If you cannot think of a time when you placed your faith in Jesus Christ, would you prayerfully consider doing so now? [ ] Yes   [ ] No

Before the death of Christ, the people had to rely on prophets, judges and priests anointed by God to intercede on their behalf. Prophets were considered the mouthpiece of God and were given the task of delivering God's Word to the people. They acted as a liaison between God and His people by instructing them in His ways. Although the people did not have personal access to the Holy Spirit as we do today, they had the privilege of witnessing many miracles and wonders at the hand of God.

WITNESS

The general theme of the Old Testament is one of a loving God continually drawing His people unto Himself. At times, His people respond to His love, turn from their wicked ways and worship Him. Unfortunately, it is only a matter of time before they are back to their old ways of worshiping the gods and idols of other nations. The cycle continues until the New Covenant is implemented with the death of Christ.

Read Deuteronomy 31:12-13.

How promising! It is possible to "learn" to fear the Lord. We see this in the Old and New Testaments. In order to do so in the Old Testament, it is necessary to look at the chronology of events that took place prior to the exodus and during the exodus. The best way to gain understanding would be to read through Exodus, Numbers, and Deuteronomy.

Stop and pray before you continue. Ask the Holy Spirit to guide you in this journey to understand the exodus and to help you learn what it is to fear the Lord.

To help you work through these books, I have listed two passages of Scripture I feel you should read. They will help you with your understanding:

1. Read Exodus 1:8-22.

Think how the Israelites must be feeling after reading this passage!

Most of us are familiar with the next scenario of events concerning the birth of Moses: the discovery of him in a papyrus basket on the edge of the river by the Pharaoh's daughter, his adoption into Pharaoh's family, and his flight to Midian after witnessing the beating of a Hebrew and killing an Egyptian. It is during this time that God reveals His plan to Moses and appoints him to deliver the Israelites out of Egypt.

Food for thought...
 • Do you think it was a coincidence that Moses was spared as a baby, raised among the Egyptians, and appointed by God to deliver the Israelites out of Egypt?
 • Is it possible that God planned the birth of Moses for this very purpose?

2. Read Exodus 3:7-10.

What is the plan? (verses 8-10)

Does this passage portray a God of love and compassion or a God of judgement and wrath?

Read Exodus 3:16-17.

Read Exodus 5:1-2, 6-14, 21.

> **"I have indeed seen the misery of my people in Egypt. I have heard them crying out because of their slave drivers, and I am concerned about their suffering"** (Exod. 3:7).

As we read on, we see where God reminds Moses of His promise and predicts pharaoh's hardness of heart. He sends Moses back with a series of plagues to convince Pharaoh to let His people go and worship their God and offer Him sacrifices. God has the foreknowledge to know that Pharaoh will not allow the people to go until the tenth and final plague.

The Passover: When the last of the plagues took place, the Israelites once again, were spared from God's wrath. He had given them specific instructions on how to insure that they would be spared from losing their firstborn to death. By sacrificing a lamb and putting its blood on the sides and top of the door frame of their home, the angel of death would know they belonged to the Lord and pass over them. Further, they were told that the Passover should serve as a day for them to commemorate and celebrate for generations to come. It would serve as a reminder of God's love and mercy in delivering the Israelites out of Egypt.

Thus, the exodus begins with an estimated two million Israelites making their way out of Egypt with their livestock, unleavened dough for the making of bread, and materials handed over to them by the Egyptians. As predicted by the Lord, they would "plunder" the Egyptians.

Imagine again you are an Israelite. Do you question God's love any longer?

You have witnessed many great acts. How will this impact your faith and the faith of your children?

Why do you think God allowed the ten plagues when He could have just disposed of Pharaoh at the very beginning?

Will you ever forget the Passover?

If "fear of the Lord" is defined as "awe and reverence toward God," do you think, like the Israelites, you are experiencing a fear of the Lord as you leave Egypt?

Now, as the Israelites are experiencing awe and reverence to God by the great miracles they have witnessed throughout the ten plagues, read Exodus 14:10 to discover their response as they witness the Egyptians coming up behind them, hemming them in before the Red Sea. Also, keep in mind that in addition to the plagues, the Lord went ahead of them in a pillar of cloud to guide them by day and in a pillar of fire to guide them by night.

In all honesty, what would your response have been?

[ ] tap your red slippers together and chant, "there's no place like home" over and over again

[ ] hold up a "will work for food" sign

[ ] grab the kids and face the Red Sea, anticipating another great miracle from God

[ ] stick up your thumb and appear to be hitch-hiking

[ ] get your last will and testament in order

[ ] scream out, "Let 'em have it Lord!"

In Exodus chapter 14, God parts the Red Sea when Moses raises his staff. To protect the Israelites from the approaching army, an angel of God withdraws from the front and goes behind them. The pillar of cloud also moves behind the Israelites and brings darkness to one side and light to the other. As the Israelites cross over, the Egyptians pursue them and the pillar of cloud throws them into confusion, causing the wheels of their chariots to fall off. Moses again raises his staff and the water sweeps over the Egyptian army. Not one of them survives.

Read Exodus 14:31 and fill in the blanks.

"And when the Israelites saw the great power the LORD displayed against the Egyptians, the people _____ _____ _____ and put their _____ in him and in Moses his servant."

What changed their attitude from one of complaining to one of reverence, awe and fear of God and His power?

"Some trust in chariots and some in horses, but we trust in the name of the LORD our God" (Ps. 20:7).

Throughout this journey, the Israelites witness great miracles, including:

- God turning bitter water to sweet water
- God raining down manna (a substance never seen before) from heaven to sustain them each day
- God providing quail so they would have meat to eat
- God bringing water from a rock
- the defeat of the Amalekites
- the descent of the Lord to the top of Mount Sinai in smoke and fire
- an angel that goes ahead of them to help defeat opposing armies
- God's wrath turned away at the request of Moses after they worshiped the golden calf
- the radiant face of Moses after he met with the Lord
- the building of the tabernacle
- the cloud that rested over the tabernacle by day and the cloud containing the fire at night

What is required to fear the Lord?

SPIRITUAL GROWTH

Here is a brief sampling of additional verses found in the Old Testament to help you understand the importance of knowing how to "fear the Lord."

"If you fear the LORD and serve and obey him and do not rebel against his commands, and if both you and the king who reigns over you follow the LORD your God—good!" (1 Sam. 12:14).

"He gave them these orders: 'You must serve faithfully and wholeheartedly in the fear of the LORD'" (2 Chron. 19:9).

"And he said to man, 'The fear of the Lord—that is wisdom, and to shun evil is understanding'" (Job 28:28).

"The fear of the LORD is the beginning of wisdom; all who follow his precepts have good understanding. To him belongs eternal praise" (Ps. 111:10).

"Do not be wise in your own eyes; fear the LORD and shun evil" (Prov. 3:7).

"Do not let your heart envy sinners, but always be zealous for the fear of the LORD" (Prov. 23:17).

Benefits to those who fear the Lord

As you are on the campus or in the world working to earn a living, think about the following benefits of learning to fear the Lord according to God's Word.

"The LORD confides in those who fear him; he makes his covenant known to them" (Ps. 25:14).

"Fear the LORD, you his saints, for those who fear him lack nothing" (Ps. 34:9).

"As a father has compassion on his children, so the LORD has compassion on those who fear him" (Ps. 103:13).

"He provides food for those who fear him; he remembers his covenant forever" (Ps. 111:5).

"He fulfills the desires of those who fear him; he hears their cry and saves them" (Ps. 145:19).

"The fear of the LORD is the beginning of wisdom, and knowledge of the Holy One is understanding" (Prov. 9:10).

"The fear of the LORD teaches a man wisdom, and humility comes before honor" (Prov. 15:33).

"The fear of the LORD leads to life: Then one rests content, untouched by trouble" (Prov. 19:23).

"His mercy extends to those who fear him, from generation to generation" (Luke 1:50).

To understand fear of the Lord read the following verses.

"My son, if you accept my words and store up my commands within you, turning your ear to wisdom and applying your heart to understanding, and if you call out for insight and cry aloud for understanding, and if you look for it as for silver and search for it as for hidden treasure, then you will understand the fear of the LORD and find the knowledge of God. For the LORD gives wisdom, and from his mouth come knowledge and understanding" (Prov. 2:1-6).

"For as high as the heavens are above the earth, so great is his love for those who fear him" (Ps. 103:11).

Encourage Your Group:
Actions for Group Study

1. As difficult as it would be to emulate the domestic qualities of the Proverbs 31 woman in present day, how would that compare to emulating her virtue of fearing the Lord?

2. What was your original definition of "fear of the Lord?"

3. When and how did you meet the Author of life (Christ)?

The Scripture that supports the CrossSeeker Covenant point of **integrity** is 2 Timothy 2:15. It states, "Do your best to present yourself to God as one approved, a workman who does not need to be ashamed and who correctly handles the word of truth."

4. How might "fearing the Lord" aid us in presenting ourselves to God as one approved?

5. God delivered the Israelites out of Egypt through Moses. Who will deliver us and how?

6. As Christians, how are we "passed over" as experienced by the Israelites?

7. Name a time when God has delivered you from your own personal Egypt.

8. Was your response to Him reverence and awe?

Re-read Numbers 11:4. The Israelites are suffering from what I refer to as selective memory. They have apparently forgotten the previous oppression they experienced in Egypt that caused them to cry out to God for deliverance.

9. Name a time when God answered a prayer, yet you found yourself suffering from selective memory. (Ex. prayed for a new job; God answered; complained about the new one.)

10. Could God have arranged for the Israelites to go back to Egypt and have their leeks, melons, fish, cucumbers, garlic and onions?

11. Selective memory could also be referred to as "whining." How does this contradict the qualities of a virtuous woman? Find a verse in Proverbs 31 to support your answer.

Between You and God

1. Would others describe you as a woman who fears the Lord?

2. Ask God to examine your desire to be a virtuous woman with worth far above rubies.

3. View your salvation (if you are a Christian) as the time you were delivered from the bondage of sin and give thanks to God.

4. Think where you might be today, had the Lord not delivered you.

5. Pray that the God of the Old Testament becomes for you a God of love.

6. Seek God's wisdom in discovering an exciting revelation for you in session 2.

7. Lift up a verse which impacted you most under "Benefits of fearing the Lord" as a praise to God.

8. Seek God's direction in what you might need to change in your life to become a woman who fears the Lord.

9. Ask God to put in your path a godly woman who can help you as you go about making these changes.

virtuous = a woman of worth

Virtuous = A Woman of Worth

As you are standing in the checkout line at the supermarket, a fashion magazine catches your eye with the subtitle, "How Do Men See You?" Or how about, "Sex Appeal: Do You Know Who He Finds Attractive?" Maybe you see, "What Men Think About Your Look" or even, "Get a Better Body—For Sex." These are actual articles that have run in the popular magazine, *Marie Claire*. In a newspaper article printed in *The New York Times*, April 4, 1999, *Marie Claire* is said to be "one of the great circulation successes of the women's magazine categories, shooting up from 400,000 in 1996 to more than twice that now." The newspaper article was entitled "Women's magazines flip past feminism—Magazine defends sex advice as part of feminism."

To sum up the article, many women's magazines that claim to embrace feminist ideology, are under attack from vocal feminists. They claim that "such magazines offer sexual advice about pleasing men as part of a larger movement toward making women feel bad about themselves, and then fixing those imagined ills in the pages of the magazines." Critics further claim that "advertisers in women's magazines have more influence than ever and don't want their ads to appear next to anything but stories about celebrity and sex."

Bonnie Fuller, the editor-in-chief for *Glamour*, defends *Glamour's* many sex articles by pointing out that sexual advice is a product of the women's movement. She further claims, "It would be unempowering for women not to be able to read about sex as much as they wanted." So let's get this straight: The feminist movement which esteems independence and sexual freedom has now evolved into a movement which encourages women to look for ways to please men, so they may feel "empowered." How ironic that in order to feel "empowered," women are now dependent on men!

In your opinion, why do you think producers, publishers, novelists, actors, and most of the forces behind media efforts, are unwilling to offer articles, books, television shows, and movies that would encourage the pursuit of virtuous qualities among women? Jot down two or three opinions you have:

1.
2.
3.

People magazine (April 12, 1999) ran a cover story on eating disorders called "Wasting Away—Eating Disorders on Campus." In the article, Traci Mann, a sociologist, is quoted as saying, "I can tell a girl that what matters is what's going on in her head and heart, but when she turns on the TV, she sees that what matters is how you look." When I first read the article, I was impressed with the noble effort exerted by *People* to tackle this growing problem. However, then I read the statement, "The idolization of wispy models and actresses adds to the problem." How ironic that *People* magazine can make this statement when it features "wispy models and actresses" in every magazine it sells!

How frightening that the self-worth of many women is molded by these worldly influences. Unfortunately, women have embraced the modified feminist ideology and will suffer long-term emotional damage through basing their self-worth on the ability to meet the world's standards. What is especially disturbing is that college women are lining up to buy these type magazines. By doing so, many will unknowingly be influenced by the agenda that is tightly woven into pages of these magazines. Add to that the influence from television, movies, and fiction novels, and you end up with a generation of women who have grown callous to God's standard to become a virtuous woman. Is it any wonder that abortion, teenage pregnancy, sexual promiscuity, sexually transmitted diseases, sexual abuse, low self-worth, anxiety disorders, depression, eating disorders, alcohol abuse, and drug abuse are all too common among women today?

Check the items below that would lend to increasing your self-worth.

[ ] losing weight	[ ] pledging a sorority
[ ] toning up	[ ] receiving compliments from men
[ ] clear skin	[ ] having really great clothes
[ ] facial beauty	[ ] driving an expensive car
[ ] having a boyfriend	[ ] making a decent income
[ ] being asked out often	[ ] leading a Bible study
[ ] many friends	[ ] being a recognized leader among
[ ] good grades	your peers
[ ] a great job	[ ] being attractive

Believe it or not, self-worth should not be dependent on any of the above mentioned items. God never intended for self-worth to be built on anything other than our standing in His Son. If our worth is based on what we do, what we look like, or what others think of us, we will be guilty of "conforming to the pattern of this world" as mentioned in Romans 12:2 rather than to the standards set forth by God.

 Now imagine standing in the same checkout line and seeing magazines with the featured articles, "How Does God See You?" or "What God Thinks About Your Look." How about, "Improve Your Body—It's a Temple"?

Would most young women buy those magazines? Why or why not?

Unfortunately, developing inner beauty is not what sells, and magazines are not about to risk profits to do the right thing.

I believe God desires a new movement among women, a movement that will dispel the world's definition of the ideal woman and spark revival for a standard God set forth long ago in His Word. Surely, the God who created us also has a plan for us. He makes no profit on the advice given in the pages of His Word and His definition does not fluctuate with the changing times.

If the Proverbs 31 woman had worth far above rubies, we too, must have worth before we can become virtuous women. For this new movement to start, women must begin to define their worth in Jesus Christ and Him alone.

Read Proverbs 31:29.

Name several women who have been praised for doing noble things:

-
-

-
-

No doubt, when I think of women who have done noble things, Princess Diana comes to mind. I can't forget her funeral and the sea of flowers left by mourners from all over the world in front of Buckingham Palace. There is certainly no question that she possessed some of the same qualities of the Proverbs 31 woman. She opened her arms to the poor and extended her hand to the needy.

Those in her household were clothed in scarlet and she in fine linen and purple. Her husband (or ex, for that matter) is respected at the city gate, where he takes his seat among the elders of the land. Upon her death, she was given the reward she had earned and her works brought her praise (and a lot of flowers!) at the city gate.

I can only help but wonder if she believed in Jesus Christ as Savior and Lord. If so, did she receive the same fanfare in heaven that she was given on earth? We certainly have no right to judge, but I think it is safe to say she was lacking one vital quality of the Proverbs 31 woman. She did not seem to fear the Lord in her last days. In the days following her death, media reports indicated that she was in transit to her boyfriend's apartment to stay the night. I imagine that if she did enter the gates of heaven, she most likely stood in awe of the virtuous women who had gone before her. Never known to the world, these virtuous women also did many noble things, but because they feared the Lord, they surpassed them all.

Think about it! What would Jesus say to women who have mistakenly built their worth by the world's standards?

One of the best illustrations of Jesus restoring worth to a woman is His encounter with the Samaritan woman at the well.

Read John 4:7-30.

> "but whoever drinks the water I give him will never thirst. Indeed, the water I give him will become in him a spring of water welling up to eternal life" (John 4: 14).

In verses 10-14, Jesus begins to explain "living water." He makes a distinction between the water in the well and living water. What is the distinction? In verse 15, the woman is extremely curious and asks him to give her living water. At that point, He tells her to go, call her husband and come back. She then tells him that she has no husband.

Jesus addresses the fact that she has no husband. Further, He points out that she has had five husbands and that the man she is currently with is not her husband. If He knew this in the first place, why did He bother to ask her to go and call her husband before He would give her living water?

[ ] He wanted to impart to her that He was more than a mere man sitting at a well.

[ ] It was necessary to address her sin before she could receive living water.

[ ] By bringing awareness to her sin, He was able to show her how desperately she needed living water.

[ ] all of the above.

In verses 28-30, she leaves her water jar, returns to her town and tells the people of her encounter. As a result, they make their way to see Jesus. Many of the Samaritans from that town believed in him because of the woman's testimony, "He told me everything I ever did" (John 4:39). The Samaritan woman had a lasting impact for generations to come.

As women, every one of us can relate to the Samaritan woman. Though we may not have committed her same sins, we have all had reason to go to the well for living water. She came to the well burdened by sin and shame, and her encounter with the living Lord left her forever changed.

Have you received Christ's offer of living water (salvation, cleansing of sin)?

Imagine if the Samaritan woman had responded to Jesus' offer of living water with, "Thanks, but I just can't take it. My sin is far too great for your living water." As absurd as it sounds, many of us are still hanging out at the well, shuffling our feet, burdened by the same shame and condemnation that brought us to the well in the first place. Some of us may have even acknowledged and received living water, but failed to actually consume it.

Have you consumed (experienced) the living water?

How comforting that Jesus did not scream at this woman and preach to her about her sinfulness. He focused on her neediness before He addressed her sinful behavior. If Christians today would follow Christ's example at the well when addressing those in sin, many would stand in line to get into our churches and hear more about living water. Jesus made His offer of living water, knowing her life would be changed forever.

Imagine yourself in this scene at the well. What brings you to the well of forgiveness?

At the well, Jesus offers to take our sin and shame in exchange for His living water—an offer we can't refuse.

Imagine going to the well and meeting one-on-one with Jesus. Tenderly, He makes an offer of living water to you in exchange for your sin and shame. You take Him up on His offer, touched that He chose to carve out time for you. In your excitement, you run from the well and race back to your home to share with everyone the significance of your encounter with the Messiah.

Samaria was impacted for generations to come because the Samaritan woman was faithful to receive living water, consume (experience) living water, leave the well and share living water with others. Will future generations be impacted by your faithfulness to do so?

There was a great price attached to living water—what an insult it would be to our Lord, to refuse His offer. No sin is too great for the living water of Jesus Christ. In exchange for living water, Jesus took our sin and carried it to the cross. There at the cross, He bore our sin upon Himself and chose to die, so that we might live. When the magnitude of what took place on the cross begins to sink in, we are forever changed. Our worth is redefined and the world pales in the shadow of the cross. Our heart is welled up with gratefulness because no one has ever loved us like that before.

When we base our worth in Jesus Christ, we live by a new standard. Until we accept His standard, it will be impossible to become the virtuous women God intended us to be.

So who exactly are you now? Read the following out loud (without Scripture references) and meditate on the significance of each one.

- I am the light of the world. (Matt. 5:14)
- I am a child of God. (John 1:12)
- Christ's life flows through me. (John 15:5)
- I am Christ's friend. (John 15:15)
- I am Christ's personal witness sent out to tell everybody about Him. (Acts 1:8)
- I am a child of God; I can call Him Father. (Rom. 8:14,15; Gal. 3:26; 4:6)
- I am a temple—a dwelling place—for God. His Spirit and His life live in me. (1 Cor. 3:16; 6:19)
- I am part of Christ's Body. (1 Cor. 12:27)
- I am a new person. My past is forgiven and everything is new. (2 Cor. 5:17)

Do you believe the things you just read? [ ] Yes   [ ] No

Which of the nine Scriptures speaks to you the most?

The Work of Satan

My husband and I have a friend who is an agent for the FBI. On a recent visit, we asked him what the most frightening experience has been in his job, and he quickly responded, "a drug bust." He went on to explain that before the bust takes place it is essential to find out every possible detail related to the subject and location of the bust, so there are no surprises. If possible, they know in advance the floor plan of the targeted location, how many occupants live there, when they come and go, weapons they possess, and any other details that would give them the advantage.

It is similar to this when we encounter Satan. We must be prepared before we go into battle and know what we are up against. What are his tactics? What weapons does he possess? How does he operate?

Examine what the following verses tell us about Satan. Jot it down.
2 Corinthians 11:14 _____
Ephesians 4:27 _____
1 Timothy 3:7 _____
John 10:10 _____

Would it make sense that Satan would desire as many women as possible to be hung up at the well of forgiveness burdened with sin and shame?
[ ] Yes   [ ] No   [ ] Not sure

How does it serve Satan if women stay at the well?

Satan would like nothing more than to render women ineffective as believers in Jesus Christ. We must recognize him for who he really is. Christian women who are burdened with shame and guilt are of no worry to him. He knows that if he can keep them at the well doubting God's love and forgiveness, they will have

41

little impact in furthering the kingdom of God. Think about it, if you are not completely free from your past, how can you race from the well with excitement to share with others this wonderful gift?

I used to think it would be nice to be able, like God, to forget my past sins. However, I have come to the conclusion that the purpose of our remembering past sin is to remind us of what Christ has done for us. It should not leave us feeling condemned, but overwhelmed with gratefulness. Once the truth of the cross begins to set in, you will never be the same again. When Jesus carried the burden of our sin to the cross, He cried out, "It is finished." Can you accept that it is finished?

Dying to Live

SPIRITUAL GROWTH

Another factor that hinders many women from leaving the well is the inability to completely die to sin and self. If this is your case, accept that you are spiritually weak and in need of spiritual growth. Many women, after receiving Christ, are enticed by the world and give in to worldly desires. If the message of the cross is not fully embraced, it is only a matter of time before they return to that which is familiar and comfortable to them. Dying to sin and self is not a one-time event. It must be a daily (or for me, moment by moment) exercise.

"For if you live according to the sinful nature, you will die; but if by the Spirit you put to death the misdeeds of the body, you will live" (Rom. 8:13).

"He himself bore our sins in his body on the tree, so that we might die to sins and live for righteousness; by his wounds you have been healed" (1 Pet. 2:24).

There are quite a few "almost dead" Christians in the world. Many are in Bible studies and serving in ministry leadership positions. They are knowledgeable about prayer and quiet times and they fill our church pews on Sunday morning. They are "almost dead" because they have given up just about everything to follow Jesus Christ, yet there is still something that masters them from time to time, causing their relationship to be less than God's best for their lives. By refusing to

When reflecting on past sin, we should be overwhelmed with gratefulness to God for all He has done.

"Those who belong to Christ Jesus have crucified the sinful nature with its passions and desires" (Gal. 5:24).

completely die daily to the sin in their lives, they miss the personal relationship and the abundant life Christ intended them to have. I speak from experience because I used to be an "almost dead" Christian, and if I'm not careful, I could be one again. The fact is, though they appear to be closer to Christ than most, "almost dead" Christians are barely alive to Christ.

Almost dead Christians are barely alive to Christ.

I believe Satan works overtime on "almost dead" Christians to keep them in bondage. One can only imagine the number of Christians with tremendous potential to impact the kingdom, who have given over to the "feel good" message of the world rather than the "do good" message of God in Christ. The irony is that nothing feels as good as choosing God's ways over the ways of the world.

As mentioned in session 2, like the Israelites, we have been delivered and passed over by the blood of Christ. Like the Israelites, we are also quick to turn away from God and return to our familiar gods.

What are some gods young people today commonly turn back to?

We make excuses for our refusal to die in order to live. Some of those excuses are listed below. Circle any you have made.

Excuses, Excuses!

- "I didn't know better."
- "That's not like me."
- "It felt so right."
- "I fell into the wrong crowd."
- "It was harmless."
- "I have low self-esteem."
- "I'm at a rough place in my life."
- "I'm a victim."
- "Don't I deserve a little happiness?"

- "I'm not ready to grow up yet."
- "No one ever taught me right from wrong."
- "At least I didn't do what so-and-so did."
- "I'm not perfect."
- "I'm trying to gain control of my life."
- "I was caught off guard."
- "Wouldn't God want me to be happy?"
- "I didn't plan for this to happen."

When we make excuses for sin, we forfeit the opportunity to have a deep and meaningful relationship with Jesus Christ.

As long as we make excuses, we will continue in sin. As long as we continue in sin, we will forfeit the abundant life and the opportunity to have a deep and meaningful relationship with Jesus Christ.

Women often come up with many excuses for staying at the well. Whether it is due to low self-worth, an inability to put the past in its place, or refusal to completely die to sin, the truth is: **to remain at the well is sin.**

In Exodus 32:26, Moses stands at the entrance to the camp and says, "Whoever is for the LORD, come to me." Jesus asks the same of us. If you have been wavering back and forth between Jesus and the world, will you come to Him? Can you find your worth in Him and Him alone? If necessary, go back to the cross and the time of your deliverance. Lay your worldly gods at the foot of the cross and commit to die to sin and self daily. Ask Him to help you experience living water and prepare you to share it with others. The women's movement God desires cannot begin unless it starts first in individual hearts. Father, let it start with mine.

Encourage Your Group: Actions for Group Study

SPIRITUAL GROWTH

The Scripture for the CrossSeeker Covenant point of **spiritual growth** is Colossians 2:6-7. It states, "So then, just as you received Christ Jesus as Lord, continue to live in him, rooted and built up in him, strengthened in the faith as you were taught, and overflowing with thankfulness."

1. How does this verse support the necessity among women to build their worth on Jesus Christ?

2. How does "overflowing with thankfulness" play a part in receiving living water, experiencing living water, and sharing living water with others?

3. What is your opinion of the "modified feminist ideology" which encourages women to please men as part of their right to sexual freedom?

4. Do the worldly influences through media impact your thinking? If so, how?

5. On the chart listed on page 36, which items did you feel would increase your worth and why?

6. When basing worth on a standard, who is more dependable: the world or God? List some reasons in your group.

7. Who were some women you listed that have done noble things, and what were their deeds?

8. What are some things that might bring college and young adult women to the well who are in need of living water?

9. How did the way Jesus dealt with the Samaritan woman impact you?

10. What are some other excuses people make to remain in sin?

Between You and God

1. As God shows you worldly influences in your lifestyle as perpetuated by the media, ask Him to help you give them up.

2. Share with God what currently defines your worth. (Be specific.)

3. Share with Christ how you felt when He took the time to meet with the Samaritan woman and shared the hope of living water with her.

4. In prayer, ask Him to do the same for you.

5. Confess to Him, have you:
   - received living water?   [ ] Yes [ ] No [ ] Not sure
   - experienced living water?   [ ] Yes [ ] No [ ] Not sure
   - shared living water?   [ ] Yes [ ] No [ ] Not sure

   If you answered, "Not Sure," let me encourage you to talk your group leader about your doubt.

6. Can you think of times when someone has shown you the kind of love that Christ exhibited to the Samaritan woman?

7. Examine your life. Have you ever been an "almost dead" Christian? Share with Christ what worldly pleasure you were hesitant to give up.

8. Read Joshua 24:14-15. Ask God to prepare you to lay your worldly gods at the foot of the cross and choose Christ. Confess to Him some "gods" you may need to give up.

virtuous = a woman of wisdom

Virtuous = A Woman of Wisdom

I'll never forget the first time I heard the name Ada Ferguson. My friend and pastor's wife, Carolyn, had been invited to be a part of a small group that was meeting weekly in Ada's kitchen. Ada was older, and the rumor was, blessed with wisdom. For weeks, Carolyn went on and on about Ada Ferguson and the godly wisdom she possessed. Finally, I could stand it no longer, and I asked if I could join the group. Prior to the first meeting, I was a little apprehensive and not sure what to expect. I pictured an elderly woman with gray hair swept up in a bun, reading Scripture aloud to us from a version of the Bible I could not understand.

Nothing could prepare me for the first meeting. When she answered the door, she was nothing like I had imagined a woman of wisdom to be. She was beautiful, stylish, and had a haircut to die for. With one son in high school and another in college, she didn't seem old enough to possess wisdom. She immediately put me at ease and we all gathered around her kitchen table with coffee in hand. She asked for prayer requests and praises and then opened in prayer. She prayed with ease and comfort, as if she was accustomed to spending many hours at the throne. She spoke to the Father with reverence, praising Him for our husbands and our responsibility as mothers to raise our children as godly seed for the next generation.

Over the weeks we met, it quickly became clear that Ada Ferguson knew God's Word backwards, forwards, sideways and upside down. Whether we were talking about husbands, politics, decorating, or how to walk daily with God, Ada had a word from Him. She could take the Scriptures and make them come alive! Her comments were always spoken with confident authority, laced with wisdom, and shared in a spirit of humility. She was not puffed up with knowledge of Scripture, but desperately dependent on walking with Christ on a daily basis. She was sensitive to sin in her life and would grieve over speaking to her husband with an insensitive tone in her voice. She would grieve over missed opportunities to share with boldness the love of Christ to someone in need. She would grieve for her children's friends that did not know the Lord or had gone astray. She spoke with compassion for everyone and instead of speaking with harsh judgement regarding another's misdeeds, she would humbly say, "All but for the grace of God go I."

CHRISTLIKE
RELATIONSHIPS

Ada looked forward to time alone with God and got up early in the morning to meet with Him. She looked for ways to please her husband and children and be a support to them. Her countenance reflected that she lived a fulfilling and abundant life. No doubt, Ada is a virtuous woman.

 Since my discovery of the Proverbs 31 passage, I had somehow imagined that to be a virtuous woman you had to tip the scale when it came to homemaking skills. Ada possessed many homemaking skills, but at the center of her life was her relationship with Christ. Ada did not possess wisdom as a result of being a good housekeeper or prioritizing her husband and children, but as a result of knowing God. The depth of her relationship with the Savior defined her role as wife, mother, friend, and mentor. I began to wonder if she had always been this way. Was it possible that she was born virtuous, as a result of inheriting some sort of "wisdom" gene?

Though Ada had been a Christian for many years, she shared how she did not really understand what it meant to make Jesus Christ the Lord of her life until her oldest child was two years old. She raised her two sons in the Christian faith and was committed to taking them to church each Sunday. At the time, Ada's husband was not a Christian, and she adopted 1 Peter 3:1-6 as her life verses, committed to winning her husband to the faith without preaching or nagging. Several years ago, Ada's husband walked forward on a Sunday morning and gave his life to Christ. God drew him that morning, but Ada's commitment 29 years ago played a large part in his name being added to the Book of Life. God honored Ada's faithful obedience and her pursuit of godly wisdom. Today, Ada and her husband minister together in their local church.

Over the years, Ada continues to have an impact on my life. I call her often just to run situations past her and gain her wisdom and insight. While many would have a tendency to share advice or personal opinion, Ada is always faithful to share pearls of wisdom and point me in the direction of the Savior.

As a result of my walk with God, I started a ministry for college women called CrossRoad Women's Ministry. God used Ada as the inspiration behind a key component of the ministry called *Titus Time*. *Titus Time* was designed to

"Then they can train the younger women to love their husbands and children, to be self-controlled and pure, to be busy at home, to be kind, and to be subject to their husbands, so that no one will malign the word of God" (Tit. 2:4-5).

emphasize the importance of mentoring, and bring awareness to the command in Titus, chapter 2, for older women to be godly examples to the younger women. For me, a mentor was essential in my quest for wisdom. By witnessing Ada's life, I had a tangible picture of the positive fruit brought forth by pursuing wisdom.

Ada is wise because: (Put a T or F on each line.)

_____she majored in Philosophy.

_____she prioritizes spending time alone with God.

_____she inherited the wisdom gene.

_____she emulates the domestic skills of the Proverbs 31 woman.

_____she commits Scripture to memory.

_____she reads fiction novels.

_____her life centers around her commitment to Christ.

_____God showed favor to her among women.

_____she finds answers to life's questions in God's word.

_____she has obtained much knowledge of Socrates, Aristotle, and Plato.

_____she reads the newspaper and watches the news daily.

_____she has a master's degree.

_____she prioritizes prayer.

_____she was voted "most likely to be wise" in high school.

Have you ever known anyone like Ada? [ ] Yes   [ ] No
If yes, who is it?

Has this person influenced your life? [ ] Yes   [ ] No
If so, how?

Is there an older woman you look up to? [ ] Yes   [ ] No
If so, does she possess the quality of godly wisdom? [ ] Yes   [ ] No

It is important to make a distinction between wisdom and knowledge. Webster's Dictionary defines "knowledge" as: "the sum of what is known: the body of truth, information, and principles, acquired by mankind."[1] "Wisdom" is defined as: "good sense: judgement."[2]

In session 1, we discovered the importance of possessing knowledge in order to abide by the world's definition of the ideal woman. From the moment we are born, we begin to store up knowledge. As we go through school, the goal is to obtain as much knowledge as possible. We are applauded for good report cards, honors classes, honor roll, and graduating at the top of our class. When we get to college, honor students are a dime a dozen and the challenge to excel is even greater. Have you ever stopped to think what the purpose is for the insatiable quest for knowledge? What is the goal? Is it to land a great job, impress our peers, make money, or what?

Charles H. Spurgeon once said, "Wisdom is the right use of knowledge. To know is not to be wise. Many men know a great deal, and are all the greater fools for it. There is no fool so great a fool as the knowing fool. But to know how to use knowledge is to have wisdom."

There is no fool so great a fool as the knowing fool.

My husband, Keith, possesses great knowledge. From the time he was in kindergarten through his senior year in high school, he made all A's and only three B's. All three B's were in handwriting. He graduated second in his high school class and went on to attend the University of Texas at Austin to pursue a degree in Chemical Engineering. During his college years, he made all A's and two B's, one of which was in a one hour Chemistry lab. He eventually graduated first in his class in Chemical Engineering and received many honors for his achievements.

One of his greatest honors came during his junior year in college when he was chosen as one of 50 students out of approximately 50,000 to receive an endowed Presidential Scholarship. Before the final cut, he was required to go before a panel consisting of the dean of each college at the University of Texas. During this interview, each of the deans asked challenging questions to help gauge the depth of knowledge each student possessed. It was a grueling and intimidating process, as the deans were seated in a semi-circle around a table facing my husband.

Toward the end of the interview, one of the deans asked my husband, "To what do you attribute your knowledge?" Without thought, my husband responded, "My knowledge is a gift from God and without Him it would be worthless." He went on to share his testimony and emphasized that his faith was far more important than his gift of knowledge. As the deans surrounding him stared back with a look of stoic expression, he remembers thinking, "I just blew a scholarship." However, on the way back to his dorm he was practically skipping with joy, having shared the truth about his source of knowledge. To this day, Keith believes that he was chosen for the scholarship because of his faithfulness in answering the question truthfully. God gave him the scholarship, not a panel of deans who, for the most part, take credit for the knowledge they themselves have acquired. My husband is gifted with knowledge, but more importantly, he is gifted with wisdom. He knows what to do with the knowledge he has been given and how to apply it in a way God would honor.

> "Blessed is the man who finds wisdom, the man who gains understanding" (Prov. 3:13).

I hope you can see where Ada and Keith have something in common. Both are filled with godly wisdom. Read the Scriptures below and pay attention to where wisdom originates and how it can be obtained. Mark the passages you like with a highlighter.

> "To the man who pleases him, God gives wisdom, knowledge and happiness, but to the sinner he gives the task of gathering and storing up wealth to hand it over to the one who pleases God" (Eccles. 2:26).

> "He will be the sure foundation for your times, a rich store of salvation and wisdom and knowledge; the fear of the LORD is the key to this treasure" (Isa. 33:6).

> "To one there is given through the Spirit the message of wisdom, to another the message of knowledge by means of the same Spirit" (1 Cor. 12:8).

> "For this reason, since the day we heard about you, we have not stopped praying for you and asking God to fill you with the knowledge of his will through all spiritual wisdom and understanding" (Col. 1:9).

The same is true for verses pertaining to knowledge:

> "For God, who said, 'Let light shine out of darkness,' made his light shine in our hearts to give us the light of the knowledge of the glory of God in the face of Christ" (2 Cor. 4:6).

> "Paul, a servant of God and an apostle of Jesus Christ for the faith of God's elect and the knowledge of the truth that leads to godliness—a faith and knowledge resting on the hope of eternal life, which God, who does not lie, promised before the beginning of time," (Tit. 1:1-2).

> "Grace and peace be yours in abundance through the knowledge of God and of Jesus our Lord. His divine power has given us everything we need for life and godliness through our knowledge of him who called us by his own glory and goodness" (2 Pet. 1:2-3).

Pop quiz! God emphasizes knowledge of what? (Check all that apply)
[ ] Ability to clone human beings
[ ] Glory of God in the face of Christ
[ ] Pi = 3.14159
[ ] Creating a space station on Mars
[ ] Our Lord and Savior Jesus Christ
[ ] Truth of the gospel message that Jesus came to save us
[ ] The latest scoop—inquiring minds want to know
[ ] Truth that leads to godliness, resting on the hope of eternal life
[ ] The ability to store tiny bits of information on a microchip

Read the verse in the margin. What surpasses knowledge?

Obviously, knowledge is not a bad thing as long as it is partnered with wisdom and used responsibly. It is far easier to possess knowledge alone, than to possess both wisdom and knowledge. In the pursuit to become a virtuous woman, it is necessary to obtain both wisdom and knowledge from the Holy One. *Wisdom is the quality that makes the virtuous woman a rare find with worth far above rubies.* Many women will possess knowledge, but only few will find wisdom. The world may esteem the pursuit of knowledge on the college campus, but God honors wisdom. Our pursuit of wisdom will impact the legacy we leave behind. Nothing the world has to offer compares to the value of wisdom. The decision to pursue wisdom, however, is our choice.

> "It cannot be bought with the finest gold, nor can its price be weighed in silver. It cannot be bought with the gold of Ophir, with precious onyx or sapphires. Neither gold nor crystal can compare with it, nor can it be had for jewels of gold. Coral and jasper are not worthy of mention; the price of wisdom is beyond rubies. The topaz of Cush cannot compare with it; it cannot be bought with pure gold" (Job 28:15-19).

> "for wisdom is more precious than rubies, and nothing you desire can compare with her" (Prov. 8:11).

> "How much better to get wisdom than gold, to choose understanding rather than silver!" (Prov. 16:16).

"I pray that you, being rooted and established in love, may have power, together with all the saints, to grasp how wide and long and high and deep is the love of Christ, and to know this love that surpasses knowledge—that you may be filled to the measure of all the fullness of God" (Eph. 3:17b-19).

Now I know these verses had to get your attention. Most women own a jewelry box to contain their treasures. For some, it may be full of silver and costume pieces, while for others it may be full of diamonds, rubies, sapphires, and design pieces. My love of jewelry started when I was a little girl. I would feed the gumball machine at the grocery store with quarters until I was rewarded with a ring, while my mother was busy shopping. I kept my trinkets in my pink jewelry box that played music when you opened the lid and a ballerina twirled around.

Never did I imagine that I would someday be up to my ears in diamonds. From the time I graduated from college, I ran a diamond business out of my home. I worked part-time during college at a jewelry wholesaler business that sold diamonds and fine jewelry to buyers representing jewelry stores across the country. While working that job, I would obtain diamonds at cost for many of my friends. After leaving that job, over the years my home business quickly grew into a thriving diamond jewelry business. I obtained accounts with diamond brokers from across the country, which would mail me diamonds upon request to show to customers. If the diamonds didn't sell, I mailed them right back. Since I did not have a store front or an inventory, the business had little overhead and I was able to sell under retail to my customers. My business went on for 12 years, until I went into part-time college ministry.

When it comes to diamonds and fine jewelry, I have seen it all. I have mailed back packages of diamonds to brokers insured for 10's of thousands of dollars. My kids think it is perfectly natural to sell diamonds across your kitchen table. When my youngest child was 4 years old, he had a friend over to play while I was showing diamonds to a customer. When his friend asked him what I was doing, he said, "selling diamonds–doesn't your mom sell diamonds?" I have seen so many diamonds over the years that I am able to grade a diamond's color and clarity without any formal training under my belt.

The amazing thing is the more diamonds I saw, the less I wanted them for myself. The reason: the more diamonds I saw, the less valuable they seemed. They weren't that rare to me. If I had a party to go to, I could borrow an extravagant piece from one of my brokers and be on my way.

This would not be possible of course, with wisdom. Wisdom cannot be bought, re-produced in synthetic form, or borrowed for an evening. It is far more valuable than any jewelry trinket money can buy, yet not many women say, "Wisdom is a girl's best friend." Most women expend more energy pursuing the worlds' valuables than seeking out the precious treasure of wisdom offered by God. The best part about wisdom is that it is free to those who ask. Every woman can afford wisdom. It has a lasting impact for generations to come. The virtuous woman has worth far above rubies because she has chosen to adorn herself with wisdom rather than rubies.

By now, if you are not convinced of the value of wisdom, you may as well check those sales flyers in the paper for a really great jewelry deal! For those who choose not to pursue godly wisdom, the Bible does not offer much support.

Many Scriptures contrast wisdom to folly. Webster's Dictionary defines "folly" as, "lack of good sense; a foolish act or idea; an excessively costly or unprofitable undertaking." [3]

Wisdom/Folly

Perhaps to your surprise, the Scriptures speak to the contrast between wisdom and folly. Here are a few for you to check out.

1) • "Discretion will protect you, and understanding will guard you" (Prov. 2:11).
   • Folly is loud, undisciplined and without knowledge. (Prov. 9:13)

2) • "Wisdom will save you from the ways of wicked men" (Prov. 2:12).
   • Folly entices others to sin. (Prov. 9:14-18)

3) • Wisdom will exalt you and honor you. (Prov. 4:8)
   • Those lacking judgement are deserving of a rod. (Prov. 10:13)

> The virtuous woman is more interested in clothing herself with wisdom than fine jewels. Truly, wisdom is a girl's best friend.

4) • "The fear of the LORD is the beginning of wisdom" (Prov. 9:10).
   • "...the mouth of a fool invites ruin" (Prov. 10:14).

5) • "The mouth of the righteous brings forth wisdom" (Prov. 10:31).
   • "...whoever spreads slander is a fool" (Prov. 10:18b).

There are many other verses which speak to wisdom and folly in Scripture. An exercise you might want to consider would be to find a Bible concordance and look up the words "wisdom" and "folly" or "fool" or "mocker" and see how many you can locate.

Proverbs 31:26 says, "She speaks with wisdom, and faithful instruction is on her tongue." In session 2, it was established that fearing the Lord is a key quality of a virtuous woman. One of the by-products that comes with fear of the Lord is wisdom, so it is not surprising that the Proverbs 31 woman spoke with wisdom. One of the best examples in Scripture of a woman who "speaks with wisdom" is Abigail. Ironically, Abigail was married to Nabal, whose name means "fool" or "wicked." The story of Abigail and Nabal is a wonderful example of the contrast between wisdom and folly. As you read the passage, keep in mind the attributes of wisdom and folly listed above.

Read 1 Samuel 25:2-42.

The story took place about 1004 B.C. when David was a fugitive from Saul. Word of his strength had gotten out and many, including Abigail, speculated the Lord would someday appoint him leader over Israel. While in hiding from Saul, he settled in the Desert of Maon and eventually found himself and his followers in need of food and provisions. David then sent ten of his men to solicit Nabal, a wealthy man living nearby, for provisions. He equipped his men with words of kindness to bestow upon Nabal and his family. David's men had never been a disturbance to Nabal before and in fact, had provided past protection to his shepherds from plunderers robbing the threshing floors. Had it not been for David and his men, they most likely would have robbed Nabal's sheepfold as well.

> **"She speaks with wisdom, and faithful instruction is on her tongue" (Prov. 31:26).**

Nabal's wife, Abigail, entered the picture when one of the servants told her the story of Nabal's refusal to help David. The servant educated Abigail as to the protection David and his men had provided them in the past.

How did Abigail respond to the servant's report? (Choose two from below).

[ ] She shared frustration over the many needy people who attempted to take advantage of their wealth.

[ ] She took 200 loaves of bread, 2 skins of wine, 5 dressed sheep, roasted grain, 100 cakes of raisins, and 200 cakes of pressed figs, and loaded them on donkeys.

[ ] She shooed them off, more concerned with what to wear to the sheep shearing party that evening.

[ ] She sent her servants ahead with provisions, and she followed behind them. She did not tell Nabal.

In verses 21-22, David shared his plan for Nabal. What was it?

After this, David came upon Abigail and she humbly bowed down before him with her face to the ground. She referred to David as her master and to herself as his servant. In verse 25, what reference did she make to David regarding Nabal?

She continued to make an appeal to David, complimenting him for fighting the Lord's battles and assuring him of God's faithfulness to fulfill His promise and someday appoint him leader over Israel. What was the first thing David said to her after her appeal? (verse 32)

In verses 33-34, David said, "May you be blessed for your good judgment and for keeping me from bloodshed this day and from avenging myself with my own hands. Otherwise, as surely as the LORD, the God of Israel, lives, who has kept me from harming you, if you had not come quickly to meet me, not one male belonging to Nabal would have been left alive by daybreak."

David then granted Abigail's request and sent her home in peace. I'm sure Abigail was experiencing a mixed bag of feelings on her way home. She must have felt tremendous relief having spared her household from death, yet great sadness in having to return to a man as wicked as Nabal. Moreover, she was likely feeling somewhat fearful at the thought of sharing her whereabouts with Nabal.

Abigail once again used good judgement and waited until morning when Nabal was sober to tell him of the harm that almost came to his household. We do not know what her exact words were, but Scripture indicates she told him "all these things." It is then that his heart failed and he became like a stone. Ten days later, the Lord struck (smote) Nabal and he died.

When David heard the news of Nabal's death, he praised the Lord for upholding his cause against Nabal and for bringing Nabal's wrongdoing down on his own head. He then sent his servants to Abigail, with the purpose of asking her to become his wife. Abigail, still true to her character, bowed down with her face to the ground and said, "Here is your maidservant, ready to serve you and wash the feet of my master's servants." Keep in mind that wealth was no stranger to Abigail, yet she humbly gave herself to David.

Abigail is a wonderful example of someone who possessed much more than knowledge. Abigail's wisdom enabled her to endure an unhappy marriage when many would have become bitter over the circumstances. Not many women today could match the integrity Abigail possessed. Most women, if faced with her situation, would have bailed out a long time ago at the bidding of family, friends, and most marriage counselors. What a testimony in a time where divorces are a dime a dozen over "incompatibility" issues. The irony is that many in the world would call Abigail the "fool" for remaining in a bad marriage. Some may even applaud Nabal's aggressive business tactics and ability to accumulate wealth. Abigail depended on God for her happiness, and as always, God prevailed.

Encourage Your Group: Actions for Group Study

1. My relationship with Ada is modeled after Titus 2:4-5, where older women are encouraged to be mentors to younger women, training them to be in pursuit of virtuous qualities. Has someone ever filled the role as mentor in your life? If so, who was it and how did they influence your life?

2. How might the world define wisdom?

3. Are most people today in pursuit of wisdom or knowledge?

4. In your opinion, do women place more value on godly wisdom or worldly knowledge?

5. On page 54, which wisdom verses had the greatest impact on you? What about the folly verses?

 The CrossSeeker statement used to support the Covenant point of **Christlike relationships** says, "In every relationship and in every situation, I will seek to live as Christ would. I will work to heal brokenness, to value each person as a child of God, to avoid petty quarrels and harsh words, to let go of bitterness and resentment that hinder genuine Christian love."

6. How did Abigail live by this principle of Christlike relationships?
   1.
   2.

7. Why do you think most people divorce today?

8. Discuss Abigail's decision to stay in an unhappy marriage.

Between You and God

1. In your pursuit to become a virtuous woman, use the chart below to identify how are you doing when it comes to the following: (Mark on the line where you feel you are at this moment in your life, with 10 being the highest level you can reach.)

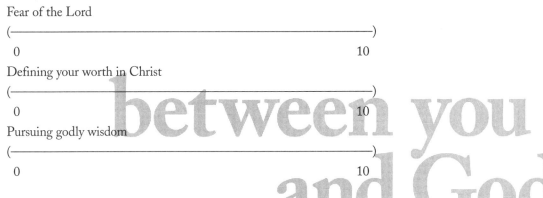

Fear of the Lord

(———————————————————————————)

0   10

Defining your worth in Christ

(———————————————————————————)

0   10

Pursuing godly wisdom

(———————————————————————————)

0   10

2. Pray to discover how a mentor (older, godly woman) might aid you in the pursuit to become a virtuous woman.

3. Ask God for the ability to experience the long-term value of wisdom.

4. Seek to understand your daily lifestyle through the wisdom of Christ. Ask yourself, would your life at present portray more of a pursuit of wisdom or folly?

5. Think of a time when you exhibited godly wisdom in a situation.

6. After reading about Abigail, share with God whether you would react as she did if given her same situation. Why or why not?

7. Re-read the CrossSeekers statement regarding Christlike relationships on page 58. Can you think of an area in your life where you need to "work to heal brokenness" or "let go of bitterness and resentment" in order to restore a relationship?

8. How can restoring a relationship bring you closer to Christ and aid you in your quest to become a virtuous woman?

Notes

1. Merriam Webster's Collegiate Dictionary, 10th ed., s.v. "knowledge."
2. Merriam Webster's Collegiate Dictionary, 10th ed., s.v. "wisdom."
3. Merriam Webster's Collegiate Dictionary, 10th ed., s.v. "folly."

virtuous = a woman of purpose

Virtuous = A Woman of Purpose

I have the privilege of meeting every other week with a small group of college women. They are a real blessing in my life and their enthusiasm for the Lord is contagious. Most of them are nearing graduation and are beginning to think about the future. They are all mature in their faith and sensitive to the leading of the Holy Spirit in their lives. Yet lately, several of them have questioned their purpose in life, or for that matter, their purpose beyond graduation. Katy is months away from receiving her teaching certificate, but has felt a nudging in recent months toward women's ministry. Emily is an older student and has recently begun to question what her motives are in finishing college. She is already in a good job, and now she is wondering if she will ever even use her degree. Each of them desires to be fully available to follow God wherever He calls and for whatever purpose He has in mind. They have invested time, money and energy heading in one direction, only to face the possibility that God may take them in an entirely different direction. As of now, they are in the "praying about it" stage and listening closely for God's leadership.

Can you relate to Katy or Emily? What are some of the struggles you are facing as a young woman? How do they impact God's purpose for your life?

Is it possible that God could interrupt our lives at any time and throw us off our plan? You bet! We are so accustomed to plotting and planning our lives that we naturally assume God will follow closely behind, blessing our human plans along the way. When Keith and I were first married, he quickly established a five-year plan to organize our lives. I still lacked a semester before graduation, and the plan called for me to work full time for several years after graduation before starting a family. This "plan" would enable us to save money for a house and get our feet on the ground financially. The plan worked great for four months, until I discovered I was expecting a child. I'll never forget the morning I took the pregnancy test. Keith was out on the porch having his quiet time, no doubt pleading with God for the test to be negative. When I stepped out on the porch and shared that I was in fact pregnant, his first words were, "You can't be pregnant. We don't have a baby in the budget." Of course, we adjusted to the new plan and now we can't imagine having done it any other way. We may not have as much money socked away, but I wouldn't trade my Ryan for all the money in the world.

What about your plans?
- Where do you see yourself in ten years?
- Why are you here?
- What is your purpose?

 Finding purpose is a common theme in life. So important is the quest for purpose that it can lead one to an abundant life or a life of misery. Unfortunately, there is not a set formula to determine one's purpose. The world has many gimmicks to aid us in defining our purpose, from career counseling to psychiatric counseling. The only problem with the world's method is that it is limited to common sense and human mortality. As Christians, we are called to look to God to define our purpose. The Proverbs 31 woman possessed three types of purpose. We will use her model to aid us in defining our purpose. How we define our purpose will also have a direct effect on our priorities.

Purpose	Priority
We have a general purpose as a child of God.	God
Most will have a purpose as a wife and mother.	Family
We have an individual purpose set forth by God.	Ministry

Discovering Your General Purpose

 As simple as it may sound, our general purpose as a child of God is to know God and make Him known. God created us in His image to be a reflection to the world of His unfailing love and mercy. Without God, the quest for purpose is futile. To know God is to know His Son. In John 14:6, Jesus states, "I am the way and the truth and the life. No one comes to the Father except through me." Many people in the world think they have cracked the code when it comes to finding purpose in life, but without Christ, their search will be in vain.

So how do we "know" Him? It is impossible to fulfill His purpose to make Him known unless we truly know Him. It is far easier to know about Him than to know Him. Christians are more adept at imparting Scripture to others than imparting the Author of the Scripture. It is one thing to gain knowledge of God,

Know Christ, know life. No Christ, no life. Without God, the quest for purpose is futile.

but entirely another to apply our head knowledge to a heart knowledge. I've heard it said that the short distance between our head and our heart can be for some, the difference between heaven and hell. We must be willing to take God's truths and apply them to our lives. We must be willing to respond to the conviction the Holy Spirit places on our heart and follow through with action. We must be willing to make Him the focal point of our lives. We must not allow anyone or anything to take the place of Christ in our lives.

Several years ago, I joined a health club at the prompting of a friend. I had to put money down for two years, but I was convinced that I would follow through with my new exercise plan. At first, I went all the time and within months, I was in pretty good shape. Well, you know the rest of the story…my life got busy and the first thing to go was the health club. I hated to pass by the club en route to somewhere else because it served as a reminder of my failed attempt to follow through with my workout plan.

As Christians, it is not enough to join the club. It is not even enough to show up at the club and listen to the trainers. We must be willing to take the advice and direction of the trainer and implement it on a regular basis or we will not see progress. The pursuit to know Christ will be in vain unless we are willing to sit at the feet of the Trainer and learn directly from Him.

Once we begin the pursuit to know Christ (the workout), He will equip us for the task of making Him known to others. As we progress in our pursuit to know Him, we can't help but share our experience with others.

When I first became a Christian in my junior year of college, I focused more on "making Him known" than knowing Him. God honored my attempts to further His kingdom, but I can't help but think how much more effective I could have been as His representative had I spent more time getting to know Him. Evangelism was an effort, and many times I had to talk myself into sharing my faith. After I married and had children, my zeal for evangelism waned and I went through what I refer to as "my apathetic years."

During those years, I often found myself mad at God. I mean, I had joined the club and served Him fervently in my initial years, so what happened? I was still attending church, reading my Bible off and on, and praying, but the spark was gone. God had called me as a speaker several years prior to my apathetic years, so I was even speaking to groups from time to time. As I look back, I now realize that I spoke from head knowledge of Scripture alone. During this time, I began to pray and specifically ask God to spark revival in my heart. Little did I know, that in order for God to spark revival in my heart, it would be necessary for me to walk the painful path of coming to the end of myself.

In the devotion book, *My Utmost For His Highest*, Oswald Chambers says, "You will never cease to be the most amazed person on earth at what God has done for you on the inside."[1]

 Now, I don't think twice about evangelism. God says in His Word, "But in your hearts set apart Christ as Lord. Always be prepared to give an answer to everyone who asks you to give the reason for the hope that you have" (1 Pet. 3:15). The message of the cross is the most powerful message in the world. When we make Jesus Christ the Lord of our life, the message of the cross becomes a reality and the gap between head and heart is bridged.

So, my general purpose is: (Check those you think I would check.)
[ ] to practice random acts of kindness and senseless beauty.
[ ] to know God.
[ ] to marry a good man, have 2.5 children and a house with a white picket fence.
[ ] to be a really good person.
[ ] to find a vocation that brings me pleasure.
[ ] to make God known to others.

discovering your
general purpose

Let's see how you do on our "Spiritual Purpose" quiz:

Circle 0 for "Not at all"; 1 for "Sort of"; and 2 for "You bet."

0......1......2   I make worship (Christian music, singing, praise, adoration) a part of every day.

0......1......2   I take thought of God throughout the day.

0......1......2   I am in the habit of consulting God when making decisions.

0......1......2   I don't freak out when something unexpected happens—I trust God.

0......1......2   When I meet someone, one of my first thoughts is, "Do they know the Lord?"

0......1......2   When I hear that someone has strayed from the faith, my first thought is to pray for them.

0......1......2   I am easily moved by praise and worship music.

0......1......2   I am anxious to spend time with God in the morning—I can't wait to see what He will show me.

0......1......2   I am burdened with the belief that the hope of our nation is Jesus Christ.

0......1......2   When someone asks my advice, I give answers based on God's Word rather than my own opinion.

0......1......2   When I hear of another's sinfulness, I remind myself that "all but for the grace of God go I."

0......1......2   I read God's Word daily. His Word provides sustenance throughout the day.

0......1......2   I praise God throughout the day.

0......1......2   When I think of the cross, my heart wells up with gratefulness.

0......1......2   I view it as a privilege to share the hope of the gospel with others.

0......1......2   I am never quite sure where God will lead me next. I often tell Him, "Whatever you want, Lord."

‾ ‾ ‾   **Totals=**

Add up your points. What does your score indicate your spiritual purpose is all about?

0-16   This is not a good place to be. Pray and ask God to spark revival in your heart. Ask God to help you get to know Him. You have personal responsibility in building the relationship with Him. It may be helpful to meet with a mature Christian for godly wisdom and counsel.

17-24   The middle ground is always a little scary. You need to move out of this category and put more energy and effort into knowing Him. You need to pray for revival to spark in your heart and the ability to be more disciplined in your quest to know Him.

25-32   Good job, but as you know, the real reward is not your score, but the result of knowing Him! Falling into this category doesn't mean you will be here indefinitely, so take precaution and always seek to know Him.

SPIRITUAL GROWTH

Hopefully your score has taught you something important about your spiritual walk. It is impossible to know God unless we are willing to set aside time for prayer, reading His Word, and worshiping Him. This is the best "workout" plan to get to know Him. Those who follow the workout plan daily will be in better shape than those who show up at the club once a week. If you fizzle out and stop the workout completely, it won't take long for consequences to set in.

Discovering Your Purpose as Wife and Mother

To become women of purpose, we must be willing to follow God's script when planning our lives. Most successful people are successful because they have a plan to reach their goals in life. Without God at the helm, we are left with our own intuition and common sense to guide us along the best path. If not God, something or someone else will play a part in defining our goals and purpose.

When you first picked up this book you may have predicted that a book about "virtuous" qualities would address specific qualities the Proverbs 31 woman possessed. When I began to write the book, I imagined that I would eventually cover the multitude of qualities inherent to this woman, but God began to show me that it was far more important to focus on a few critical qualities that led to her virtuous standing.

To become a virtuous woman, it is essential to focus on becoming a woman who fears the Lord, a woman who bases her worth in Jesus Christ, a woman who pursues godly wisdom, and a woman who is walking in her God-given purpose. If this is done, the remaining virtues will come as an outflow of her established relationship with Jesus Christ. Women who possess virtues, yet lack the foundation of a deep relationship with Christ, will fall into the category of "women who do noble things" (Prov. 31:29). Anytime we attempt to do anything in our own strength we are at a greater risk for failure.

It is important to note that I am not just referring to non-Christian women. Many Christian women will fail to reach the status of a woman who surpasses them all because they lack the essential key element of a thriving relationship with Jesus Christ. Notice the word, "thriving." To thrive is to grow or flourish. There are many Christian women who are stagnant in their faith, but for all practical purposes, have mastered many of the qualities of the Proverbs 31 woman. In generations past, it was not uncommon for mothers to teach their daughters virtuous qualities, but many did not possess the right motives when training them.

What are some "virtuous qualities" you remember being taught?

Serving in college ministry, I often talk to college women who are in pursuit of all the world has to offer. Many of these women witnessed discontented mothers who were not seeking God's purpose for their lives. How unfortunate, that so many mothers with good intentions failed to pass on to their daughters the one thing that really matters: the value of a deep and intimate relationship with Jesus Christ. From that relationship alone comes joy, no matter what our given purpose in life.

In my early meetings with Ada, I remember her talking often of the importance of finding joy in all we do. She made it clear that our joy must come from our love of Christ and willingness to serve Him. Because I had not yet defined my worth solely in Christ and was still influenced by the wisdom of the world, I was simply going through the motions in my pursuit to become virtuous. It didn't take long before I became frustrated with the whole pursuit. I was attempting to follow God's standard in my own strength. I would think of Ada's advice, "Whatever you do, work at it with all your heart, as working for the Lord, not for men" (Col. 3:23). When my kids would spill juice on my newly mopped floor (mopped with attempted joy in my heart), I would try singing, "The Joy of the Lord is my Strength" over and over to brainwash myself while cleaning up the mess. The Proverbs 31 woman modeled that the joy of the Lord was her strength, and she didn't just sing about it, she lived it.

When defining our purpose as a wife and mother, God has given us some basic principles to abide by in His Word. The majority of college women will marry at some point in their lives, and logically, their purpose as a woman will change. The world leads many to believe that this is not necessary and that purpose can only be found by achieving that which is most rewarding to our worth and esteem. The world sends a message that tells us to look out for number one and take care of our own needs first. Many women buy into this message without question, until they marry and have children. At that point, it becomes more difficult to look out for number one when there are little ones in the picture who have also determined themselves to be number one. Thus the conflict begins.

As many college women read this, I predict that some will sigh heavily and say, "Oh no, not the career, family conflict." I want to be very honest at this point. I have spent many hours in prayer over this portion of session 5. I have debated

> **A mother's greatest calling is to pass on to her children the value of a deep and intimate relationship with Jesus Christ.**

long and hard over what to say, how much to say, and how to say it. God has been faithful to give me morsels of His truth, backed by Scripture and personal testimony. Because most college women will go on to marry and have children, and thus spend the majority of their years as a wife and mother, it is prudent to address a woman's primary purpose after marriage. *It is no different than having long-range goals and developing a strategy to assist you in achieving your goals.* It would be unwise to make decisions based on the here and now, without taking the future into consideration. So what is the primary purpose of a virtuous woman who is married with children?

There is no way to study the Proverbs 31 woman without addressing her commitment to family. Out of twenty verses (11-30) that extol her virtuous qualities, nine verses deal specifically with her husband and/or children. The remaining eleven verses deal with qualities that indirectly benefit her family and help stabilize the home environment. They include: sewing, investing, helping the needy, selling garments, and her attributes of wisdom, strength, dignity, and fear of the Lord. Only three verses specifically address "work for profit" activities she accomplished. These are Prov. 31:16; 31:18, and 31:24. Take a look at them.

This woman is no sluggard. She is a go-getter in everything she does and rarely has time for herself. She is constantly putting the needs of others before her own needs. She doesn't look for ways to spend her money (ouch), but instead she invests it. To be honest, never in the passage does it clearly state that a woman should not have a full-time career along with a family. However, it is apparent that the Proverbs 31 woman did not go outside the home to find full-time work.

The Proverbs 31 Purpose

"Her husband has full confidence in her and lacks nothing of value. She brings him good, not harm, all the days of her life" (Prov. 31:11-12).

Who does she seek to bring good to: her husband or herself?

"She watches over the affairs of her household and does not eat the bread of idleness" (Prov. 31:27).

Who is in charge of household matters?

"Her children arise and call her blessed; her husband also, and he praises her: 'Many women do noble things, but you surpass them all'" (Prov. 31:28-29).

Who arises and calls her blessed?

[ ] Her husband and kids   [ ] Her best friend

[ ] Her boss   [ ] Her pastor

[ ] Her co-workers   [ ] Her clients

From this passage, who or what is most important to the virtuous woman?

When it comes to addressing the career/family controversy, I must admit that I am probably not the best source for giving fair and unbiased advice. God has shown me personally, that I cannot work a full-time job and devote the necessary hours to my husband and children. Even with my home-based diamond business, there were times when work was heavy and it would begin to take a toll on the family.

In preparing for this session, I mentioned to my husband one evening that it would be nice to have a testimony from a mother who works full time, yet also sincerely desires to be an ideal wife and mother. A few days later, I picked up the newspaper (Austin American Statesman, April 22) and a story on the front page of the business section caught my eye. It read, "Shop owner closing store to be with family." The article went on to say that the owner of a prestigious bridal salon had decided to shut the doors and walk away from her $1.5 million-a-year shop during its second most successful year in the ten years she had owned the shop. The article further stated, "For Susan Martin, like many businesswomen who have long juggled careers with children, family is taking precedent over work." I couldn't believe my eyes. It was apparent that God wanted me to see the article. I prayed about it and then I picked up the phone and called the bridal shop. I told her assistant that I was interested in interviewing her for a book I was writing for college women. Her assistant relayed the message, and Susan called me that day. I asked her over the phone if there was anything specific that led up to her decision to close her shop. She replied, "About three years ago, in the midst of great stress associated with trying to do it all, I became a born again Christian." Here are some highlights of her interview:

Question #1: What brought you to the decision to stay home full time with your children?

It took a combination of many things to convince me to change my ways, my thinking, and my heart. I was broken, not on the outside (I was doing all the world approved of), but on the inside. I was frustrated, angry, exhausted, lonely, and disappointed. I felt unappreciated, overworked, and totally tapped out with nothing left to give. My frustration came from a feeling I carried with me most of the time, a feeling that I was never in the right place at the right time. If I was at work, my children needed me, and if I was at home my business and employees needed me. If I was doing work at my business or doing something for the kids, then my husband needed me for business or personal reasons. There was always a crisis at the place where I wasn't. I felt terribly pulled in many directions, unable to perform to the expectations of those around me. Would I regret in ten years the choices I was making now? What did God expect of me? Who's approval was I seeking, His or others? Slowly, God began to show me that it wasn't necessary to perform because He loves me for who I am and not what I do. He gave me the ability to see myself through His eyes and the strength to value my relationship with Him and my family above what the world holds important.

I decided I would do whatever it took to follow His leading. The first and most logical step was to work less and be at home more. The more I was at home, the more I wanted to be home. The tables totally turned. Before, I saw the children (as much as I loved them) as being very needy and a burden and inconvenience (someone sitters could take care of). Now I saw work as the burden and inconvenience, and it became very clear that no one should be raising my children but me! I felt proud to claim that I was my children's mom!

Question #2: What advice do you have for college women in regard to balancing a full-time career with raising a family?

When you decide to have children, really decide to have them and enjoy them and get involved in their world. Don't make them an extra as I did, adding them as an addition to your career. Don't make them fit into a career world where it is impossible for them to be your first priority. See them as the incredible God-given gift that they are, worthy of your undivided attention. They will bring you more joy, more reward, more happiness and more sense of accomplishment than any career available.

Question #3: The world tells women they can do it all. What is your verdict?

This deception clouds the decision-making process a young woman experiences when facing the career/family conflict. The consequences on the family are everywhere you look today in our society. The standard from which we are to compare ourselves in the 90's is false, and many are suffering consequences from trying to live up to this lie.

We may have to choose to live with fewer material goods. It is foolish to invest our energies into acquiring "treasures on earth" if we are forfeiting "treasures in heaven."

Question #4: How do your husband and children feel about your decision to close the shop?

They love it! My husband has been incredibly patient through all this soul-searching and has encouraged and supported me all the way. This is what he has always wanted from the time our first child was born. He never pressured me because he wanted me to be happy. I bought into the world's idea of what makes a modern woman happy, and all it did was make me more unhappy as each year progressed. So much for what the world tells us.

My children love it too, and I now feel like I actually have a relationship with each one. Before, I felt as if I was losing them, especially my eldest child. I loved my children dearly but I was not a part of their lives. Children adapt to even the worst of conditions, and my children adapted while I was working, like any other child of a working mother. But is that the best situation for them? Only time will tell, and I have personally decided not to take the chance. You can't turn back time.

Personal Impact

CHRISTLIKE RELATIONSHIPS

Susan Martin is as close as it comes to the world's definition of an ideal woman. She is beautiful, slender, assertive, savvy, independent, and extremely successful. She knew what she wanted and she went after it. She attempted to be a part of her children's lives and involved herself in their many activities. Yet, in the end, she felt empty and confused. After becoming a Christian, God began to gently show her what had lasting value in her life. In the end, God prevailed and Susan chose to lay her successful business career at the foot of the cross, obedient to the conviction Christ laid on her heart. She chose doing good over feeling good. She chose Jesus over the world. Does she have any regrets? If you ask her, she'll tell you her only regret is that she didn't do it sooner.

Do you think she's nuts for closing her shop? [ ] Yes   [ ] No

Many college women have failed to look to God and His Word when defining their purpose. When this happens, women are left to their own instincts and desires or the counsel of others. The world stresses that we are in charge of our own destiny, yet Scripture contradicts that belief. As Christian women, we must resist the habit of planning our own lives. This is imperative for college women because they are in a season of life where many decisions are made that could produce consequences that affect their lives for years to come.

As Christian women, we must resist the habit of planning our own lives.

It is against God's will to determine our path without consulting Him.

Titus 2:3-4 says, "Likewise, teach the older women to be reverent in the way they live, not to be slanderers or addicted to much wine, but to teach what is good. Then they can train the younger women to love their husbands and children, to be self-controlled and pure, to be busy at home, to be kind, and to be subject to their husbands, so that no one will malign the word of God."

This verse emphasizes the importance of older women training the younger women to:
  [ ] fight for equal rights and burn their bras in the streets.
  [ ] climb the career ladder and prioritize their job.
  [ ] love their husbands and children.
  [ ] find a quality day care for their children.
  [ ] be busy at home.
  [ ] insist on equal rights in the home.
  [ ] wear the pants in the family.
  [ ] be subject to their husbands.

So important is this command in Titus 2 that it ends with a warning, stating that to not follow this standard would be to "malign" the Word of God. Webster's defines "malign" as "to act maliciously: to speak evil of."[2] I realize that there are many godly women who desire to be full or part-time homemakers, but due to unfortunate circumstances, it has become necessary for them to work full time. My heart breaks for these women and as Christians, we should be in the habit of interceding on their behalf with prayer. For these women, it is important that their children know their heart's desire in regard to being home. These children will probably fare better than children who have mothers who stay home full time, but resent their role and complain bitterly.

In conclusion to the career/family conflict, let me say that it is most important to individually seek God's counsel when making a decision. A woman who fears the Lord, defines her worth in Christ, and pursues godly wisdom, cannot go wrong in defining her purpose. This woman by her very nature is dependent on Christ in every area of her life.

Discovering Your Individual Purpose

Our individual purpose will be defined within the context of our general purpose of knowing God and making Him known. Our individual purpose is a specific purpose that God has for us using the gifts and talents He has blessed us with. Regardless of what our gifts and talents are, they should be used for the ultimate purpose of furthering God's kingdom. Whether we are a student, in a vocation, in full-time ministry, married, or a parent, our individual purpose should be utilized within the context of our lives. Though our gifts and talents will most likely remain the same, our individual purpose or assignments will change from time to time. If we have sincerely embraced the general purpose for our lives, then our individual purpose will come as a by-product of our pursuit to know Him.

Read Matthew 28:18-20. This passage is referred to as the Great Commission, and we are told to go and make _____ of all nations. When we become His disciples we assume the responsibility of making Him known to others (making disciples), and caring for His flock. What an awesome task!

Encourage Your Group:
Actions for Group Study

1. As a college student, what kind of plans have you made for the future?

2. Did you seek God's counsel in regard to your plans?

3. Discuss with your group the importance of knowing God and making Him known.

4. Discuss among your group the "Knowing God Self-Test" and some solutions to know Him more.

5. What can college women do to better prepare for the possible calling of becoming a wife and mother?

 The CrossSeeker Covenant point that supports **service** states, "I believe that God desires to draw all people into a loving, redeeming relationship with Him. As His disciple, I will give myself to be His hands to reach others in ministry and missions."

6. How does this support a woman's general purpose to know God and make Him known?

7. Have you given yourself completely to be His hands in ministry and missions? If not, would you consider doing so now?

8. Discuss among your group Susan Martin's decision to end her working career and become a full-time mother.

Between You and God

1. Share with God how how you would feel if He began to direct you down a different path than the one you are currently on.

2. Pray that God will help you define a current "workout" plan to get to know Him better.

3. Discuss with a godly woman in your church your thoughts about the interview with Susan Martin. Ask for her opinion in regard to the career/ family conflict.

4. Ask for God's guidance as you seek to have a vocation that brings you pleasure or the opportunity to stay home full time with your children.

5. Ask God to show you ways to be responsible with the gospel message He has entrusted to you.

Notes

[1] Oswald Chambers, *My Utmost for His Highest* (London, England: Simpkin, Marshall Ltd., 1927)

[2] *Merriam Webster's Collegiate Dictionary,* 10th ed., s.v. "malign"

virtuous dating

Virtuous Dating

She sat across my kitchen table sobbing uncontrollably and mumbling, "please help me—I have to get him back." I remember when I received the phone call late one evening from a college girl who is close to our family. She asked me to talk with one of her friends who was desperate after a break up with her boyfriend. Her friend was so desperate, she was willing to drive 45 minutes and talk with a woman she had never met before. I figured it was one of those divine appointments that only God can arrange, so I told them to head on over. My heart broke for her as she shared detail after detail of an abusive and unstable relationship that had just come to an end. The worst part was that she was dead set and determined to get him back. It was so difficult to keep from grabbing her shoulders and saying, "Are you nuts?! This guy is a loser, so count your lucky stars the relationship is over and you didn't marry him!" I had to continually remind myself that I, too, had experienced my share of unhealthy relationships during my college years.

I let her cry for awhile, and then I turned the conversation and asked her, "Do you think this guy is God's best choice for you?" I went on to share how God loves her more than anyone and that He wants what's best for her. She continued to ask how she could survive without having him in her life and I pointed out that sometimes God allows things (like a break up) to get our attention and draw us closer to Himself. She had given up everything for this relationship. They were in the habit of spending every waking moment together. In her weakness, she was able to admit that her esteem was at an all time low as a result of this relationship. Yet, she was willing to continue in a dysfunctional relationship rather than face the ultimate—being ALONE.

She claimed she had never thought about God having an opinion in regard to who she dated. She had a limited understanding of God's love, so I explained to her how God proved His love when He sent His Son to die for us. I went on to share how she could begin a new life by placing her trust in Him. With Christ, she would not be alone. She eagerly expressed a desire to receive the living water of Jesus Christ, and I had the privilege of leading her to Christ that evening across my kitchen table. She was no longer crying. She was anxious to get back to her dorm and start reading the Bible I had given her.

Sometimes God allows things (like a break up) to get our attention and draw us closer to Himself.

A deep and personal relationship with Jesus Christ can satisfy the longing in any heart to be loved and accepted.

"For everything in the world—the cravings of sinful man, the lust of his eyes and the boasting of what he has and does—comes not from the Father but from the world. The world and its desires pass away, but the man who does the will of God lives forever" **(1 John 2:16-17).**

Several months later, I received the news that she was in a new relationship, but this time with a married man. My heart broke to hear that once again, she had replaced the perfect love of Jesus Christ with something that would leave her empty and miserable in the end. Unfortunately, this relationship would affect other innocent lives. What happened? What went wrong? We could easily focus on her lack of discipleship or failure to attend church in the months that followed her decision. We could even speculate that she didn't really mean it when she prayed to trust Christ as her Savior. Although these are all possibilities, one thing is certain: She was unable to believe that a deep and personal relationship with Jesus Christ could satisfy the longing in her heart to be loved and accepted. She chose the easy way out. A deep and intimate relationship takes time—it does not happen overnight. It is a process. She was not willing to go through the awkward "getting to know you" stage with Jesus.

Many college women, like the one above, enter relationships based on emotion. They give very little thought to the long-term consequences of giving their heart, soul, and body to someone who most likely will not become their husband. Without God in the picture, they are left to their own intuition and emotion to guide them in the relationship. Christian women are not exempt from making poor choices when it comes to dating, and some will compromise previous commitments made to God in order to experience what they deem to be love. The desire to be loved and accepted is intense, and not many realize that God can fill the empty and hollow places within them. We are in a pleasure-driven world that is accustomed to instant gratification. How can God match that? Because it takes time to build a deep relationship with Christ, many will bail out early in the game without ever giving Jesus a chance, while others will never know there was a game in the first place.

College women who are in pursuit of becoming virtuous women must commit to a different standard of dating—they must commit to "virtuous dating." So what is virtuous dating?

Let's start by defining what it is NOT:

Virtuous dating is not "dating for fun."

Dating for fun is common in the college years and usually has no set standards in place. The main goal is to make sure you are not home alone on the weekends. Many girls date for fun to ensure they have a date to an upcoming party, football game, or weekend activity. Often, they accept a date for lack of a better offer. Simply put, it's dating for the sake of dating. While dating for fun may seem innocent enough, it is not sincere in its motives and can lead to damaged emotions. So why is it so common? Our culture dictates the social mores of dating. Dating signifies acceptance and validates a person's worth. For those who mistakenly base their worth on the acceptance of others, dating is a temporary boost to the esteem. It says, "I am not rejected." This need to be accepted can lead many women to compromise in the physical aspects of the dating relationship. *Virtuous dating does not base its worth on the acceptance of another person. The virtuous woman sees herself holy and acceptable in the eyes of God because of her standing in Jesus Christ.*

Virtuous dating is not "dating by emotion."

Many women are guilty of dating by emotion and trusting their own instincts to guide the relationship. Because the relationship is based on emotion and emotions tend to waver, it is not built on a stable foundation. It is based on statements like, "I just have this feeling he's the one," or "it feels so right when we kiss." Many women fall into the trap of dating by emotion because they are desperate for a standard to gauge the relationship. For many, listening to emotion is easier than learning to listen to God. The problem comes when the feelings are gone and confusion shortly sets in. What seemed so right in the beginning, may not seem so right a year later. The damage is done when emotional and physical intimacies have been exchanged that should have been reserved for marriage. *Virtuous dating does not get carried away by emotion, but is based on the firm foundation set forth in God's Word.*

The damage is done when emotional and physical intimacies have been exchanged that should have been reserved for marriage.

Virtuous dating is not "joined at the hip dating."

Many dating relationships evolve into serious, long-term relationships that emulate marriage. These couples are joined at the hip and do everything together. Their schedules revolve around the relationship and each other. They have given up friends and social activities to be with one another. They study together, eat together, shop together, and sometimes sleep together or even live together. Many women crave this type of relationship to fill a void formed by unmet needs in their lives. Some women, upon ending this type of relationship, will immediately move into another long-term relationship, almost like a drug addict seeking a "fix." *Virtuous dating places God first in the relationship, thus eliminating the possibility of being joined at the hip. The relationship is not the focus, but instead the personal relationship with Christ.*

Virtuous dating is not "mission field dating."

Many Christian women will loosen their standards and go out with an unbeliever, assuming that if the relationship progresses they will have an opportunity to win their date to the Lord. While that is a noble consideration, there is too much at stake to make presumptions about another's salvation. If there is an emotional connection (and you can count on the devil's encouragement), all rationality flies out the window and standards are compromised for the sake of "love." Many women will continue in the relationship, convinced that their own passionate belief in Christ will influence their partner and bring him to Christ. While this is occasionally successful (remember Ada), dating is not the proper platform to experiment with another's salvation. A friendship relationship would be more conducive and less emotionally entangling than a dating relationship. *Virtuous dating prioritizes the spiritual needs of others above the individual need to be in a relationship. A virtuous woman does not become unequally yoked with unbelievers. (2 Cor. 6:14)*

A virtuous woman does not become unequally yoked with unbelievers. (2 Cor. 6:14)

The Biblical Standard

In all honesty, dating is never mentioned in the Bible. Dating is something that is standard to our culture and did not take place in Bible times. Each Christian will need to evaluate what their definition of dating is, as well as their purpose for dating. Virtuous women will need to take their proposed standard before God and seek His approval. For some, dating will be a stumbling block in their relationship with Christ, and it will be necessary to find an alternative to dating. Others may have success with dating and not find it to be a hindrance to their personal walk with Christ. I am certainly not saying that dating is wrong. Most people who are married dated their spouse at some point. The question is: Can you be in pursuit of becoming a virtuous woman and date responsibly? I believe it is possible for women who fear the Lord, base their worth wholly in Christ, pursue godly wisdom, and prioritize knowing God and making Him known.

In the college group I meet with, one of the girls recently mentioned that she has made the decision to put dating on a back burner. She admitted that she is easily swayed by emotion that could lead her into temptation and throw her off course in her walk with Christ. I appreciate her spiritual maturity in being sensitive to the Holy Spirit's leading in her life. This is not to say she will never date again, but her focus is relying on God, building her relationship with Christ, and waiting for His permission to resume dating.

What is your dating profile? Have you ever fallen into any of the four categories mentioned previously? If so, was it difficult to prioritize your relationship with Christ?

Let's examine why you date (short or long-term). Check all that apply:

[ ] Never thought about it–if he's decent, I say "yes."

[ ] I'm on the lookout for Mr. Right.

[ ] How else will I find someone to marry?!

[ ] I crave physical intimacy and hearing someone say, "I love you."

[ ] I consult God before accepting a date or dating someone seriously.

[ ] To not date, would be REJECTION.

[ ] It's great to have someone to do things with.

[ ] I'm tired of eating pizza in the dorm lobby with my friends on Friday night.

[ ] I want a guaranteed date to all social activities. No more waiting by the phone.

[ ] Dating for me is the result of a friendship that God has allowed to progress.

[ ] Always a bridesmaid, never a bride! When will it be my turn?

[ ] I have to date to see if I get the magical "this is the one" kind of feeling.

[ ] Prince Charming doesn't just show up on your doorstep.

[ ] Let me get this straight: holding hands, smooching, and endearing words OR staying home and watching Seinfeld re-runs? It's a no-brainer.

Now that you've examined your reasons for dating, it is time to ask:

What's Your Plan?

What are your standards for physical intimacy in a dating relationship? Many women will stumble (if not fall) in this area for lack of a plan. Not many women would go into a big job interview without anticipating certain questions and rehearsing the answers, yet women go on dates without ever anticipating what might take place. When I taught middle school girls in the youth group and we would discuss the hot topic of remaining pure, the girls would respond with wide-eyed innocence and insist that they would NEVER give up their virginity. Of course, none of them were allowed to date and this protected them from many tempting circumstances. I commended them for their commitment to remain pure, but warned them that they better come up with a plan. It's too late for a plan if you happen to find yourself in the backseat of a car with the windows fogging up and a guy whispering sweet-nothings in your ear.

When determining a standard for physical intimacy, it is good to think ahead and ask yourself, "What actions, if they were to occur, would I feel conviction over? If Jesus were on the date, what would He consider appropriate?" The Holy Spirit will guide you in developing an appropriate standard for physical intimacy when given a chance.

Isaiah 32:8 says, "But the noble man makes noble plans, and by noble deeds he stands."

What Is Virtuous Dating?

What's your plan when dating? A virtuous woman will have a plan when it comes to dating. She will know in advance what her standards are for accepting a date, going on a date, and entering a dating relationship. A virtuous woman will not focus on "looking" for a guy. She will trust God to be the matchmaker and wait on His timing. God may choose to use a date to bring two people together, but the virtuous woman will be sensitive to this and recognize the voice of God over emotion.

Accepting a date

A virtuous woman will have established a friendship with the suitor and know his spiritual standing. If he is an unbeliever, a date is out of the question, but the friendship may continue. If there is any concern of temptation, she may suggest that they go out in the company of another godly couple. This will make the date less awkward and ensure built-in accountability for all parties. She will pray about it before accepting a date. If she knows up front that God is not leading her to go out, she will tell him in a spirit of love and encourage a continued friendship. The virtuous woman is much more selective when it comes to accepting a date, so she may not go out as much as other college women.

It's too late for a plan if you happen to find yourself in the backseat of a car with the windows fogging up and a guy whispering sweet-nothings in your ear.

A virtuous woman will know in advance what her standards are for accepting a date, going on a date, and entering a dating relationship.

Going on a date

CHRISTLIKE
RELATIONSHIPS

Once a virtuous woman has prayerfully decided to accept a date, she will spiritually prepare herself for the date. She will know in advance what (if any) physical contact is permissible. Her suitor will be aware of her standards by the simple fact that she is virtuous. However, it may be necessary for her to spell it out if there appears to be any confusion while on the date. The purpose of the date is to get to know each other better. Just as in any relationship, God commands us to love our neighbor as we love ourselves (Matt. 19:19b), so the date will serve as an opportunity to model God's love.

Entering a dating relationship

The virtuous woman will not enter into a serious dating relationship unless God is leading in that direction. Because she is in the practice of being selective when choosing a date, we can assume that there is great potential for engagement if it has reached the "serious dating" level. The virtuous woman is not interested in wasting her time with a long-term relationship that provides nothing more than companionship and runs the risk of damaged emotions if a break up occurs. Before she commits to a serious relationship, she has come before God in prayer and sought His counsel. In addition, she may have enlisted the godly wisdom and counsel of another Christian, who is mature in the faith and familiar with the relationship. This helps to ensure that the relationship is not driven by "emotion," but rather by wisdom.

So what if I'm not a virgin? Do I forfeit my chance to pursue virtuous dating?

PURITY

Let me answer this by saying that I am a living testimony that it is never too late to pursue virtuous dating. When I became a Christian at the age of 21, I was more than willing to follow godly principles in my dating relationships. With a changed heart comes a changed life and I was ready for a change. Many women feel they don't deserve a godly man if they have given up their virginity. This is not true. My husband saved himself for marriage, and though I cannot claim the same, as a couple we were committed to purity. We had built a strong friendship before we entered a dating relationship. When we made the decision to formally date, we both knew in our hearts that engagement would follow. Throughout our dating relationship, we continued to look to God for

> "Therefore, if anyone is in Christ, he is a new creation; the old has gone, the new has come!" (2 Cor. 5:17).

direction. We even agreed that we would not say the words, "I love you," unless we were engaged. We knew that once those magical words were exchanged, an emotional link would be established within our hearts. One evening he brought me flowers, and when I read the card it said: "I love you very much. Will you marry me?" Words cannot express how special it was to wait on God and His timing.

What type of man does a virtuous woman marry?

Regardless of whether or not you are currently dating, you should be thinking about what kind of man God might desire you to marry. I'm not talking about a specific checklist of characteristics, but basic qualities of a godly man. Once this is established, there is little sense in bothering with one date if the person who has asked you out does not meet the basic criteria. It is similar to signing up for upper division courses in college. Sometimes there is a prerequisite that is required before you can qualify to take the class. When you reach "virtuous" status, your knowledge and understanding of spiritual matters will fall into upper division standing. If you register for Organic Chemistry, but are accidentally placed in Basic Chemistry 301, imagine the frustration in having to go back to the basics again. Further, imagine the confusion for a student with Basic Chemistry knowledge, who is accidentally placed in an upper division Organic Chemistry class.

SPIRITUAL GROWTH

When you establish a deep and personal relationship with Jesus Christ, with it comes the responsibility to abide by God's terms. It would not be prudent to carry on a dating relationship with someone who is less mature in the faith. This is especially true for Christian women, who run the risk of marrying someone who is weaker in the faith and not accustomed to being a spiritual leader.

So what is the basic criteria?

A virtuous woman should not enter into a long-term dating relationship with, get engaged to, or marry a man who is not:

A believer: At some point in his life he has placed his trust in Jesus Christ and speaks openly about his salvation. He is prepared to share with others the hope of Christ that resides within his heart. (2 Cor. 6:14)

Submissive to God: He is reliant on God to assist him in making decisions. He is in the habit of reading God's Word on a regular and consistent basis, and prayer is a part of his everyday life. He will exhibit the fruit of obedience to God's direction in his life. Spending time with God is his sustenance to make it through each day. (Eph. 5:25)

A spiritual leader: He is comfortable leading in prayer and giving godly counsel and instruction based on principles in God's Word. He is confident in his salvation and desires to grow in his faith. He is committed to attending church and obediently gives a portion of his income to the local church. (Scripture indicates a minimum of 10%.) He recognizes that everything he has belongs to God. (Eph. 5:23)

A provider: He recognizes the God-given responsibility of a husband to provide for the basic needs of the family. However, there must be a healthy balance in his attitude toward "providing" income for his family or he may run the risk of becoming a workaholic. There are many men who "provide" financially for their families, yet lack the commitment to prioritize their family over their jobs. A Christian man who is submissive to God's leading will prioritize meeting the spiritual, emotional, and physical needs of his family.

A protector: He recognizes his responsibility to fulfill the role of protector to his family. Next to God, his family is his second highest priority. If need be, he would lay down his life for his wife and children to protect them. He is others-centered rather than self-focused. (1 Pet. 3:7)

Not only is it critical that a man possess the basic criteria for a godly man, but it is also necessary that he exhibit behavior that indicates he will "walk his talk." For example, before Keith and I were married, we decided that when we had children, it was important for me to stay home. When we first married, I had a pretty good job and it was tempting to factor my income into our expense budget. I begged him to consider my income when purchasing furniture for our new home. There was a one-year, interest-free plan available, so my income would have enabled us to buy more furniture up front. I mean, why not? The "plan" was for me to work for several years, so it made logical sense (to me) to accumulate the furniture we needed on these one-year credit plans. Keith held firm to his commitment to never depend on my income for expenses and to treat it as "extra." This served as one of my first lessons in the necessity to submit to your husband! Of course, you know the rest of the story: I ended up pregnant within four months of marriage and on top of that, went into early labor and was ordered to bed-rest. I was able to work only four months in total! My husband took his responsibility as provider very seriously and because of his commitment, his wisdom paid off.

I believe the pendulum is swinging back to an era where mothers desire to be the primary caregivers of their children. The long-term results of the women's movement are beginning to play out as many children of working mothers desire more for their own children. Don't let the world fool you. No matter how much you spend on childcare or how exceptional the childcare arrangement is, there is absolutely no one who will love your child as you would. Quality moments with your children don't just happen after 5:00 P.M. In fact, 5:00 P.M. is arsenic hour in our home because everyone is hungry, tired, and cranky. Children are a blessing from the Lord, and God never intended for us to farm them out for others to raise. God's heart is tender toward mothers who encounter situations where they are forced to work, but many women today are choosing to work, convinced that a vocation will lead to greater fulfillment. I can imagine no greater fulfillment than the privilege of spending quality and quantity time with my children.

A virtuous woman will not enter into a serious dating relationship, get engaged to, or marry a man who is not supportive of her desire to be a full-time mother. There are many men who would rather have a bigger home, a nicer car, and other pleasures of life afforded by two incomes, than a wife who stays home full time with the children. Like the Proverbs 31 woman, virtuous women will plan for the future and not be swayed by human emotion.

A virtuous woman "watches over the affairs of her household" (Prov. 31:27). God intended for women to be the facilitator of relationships in the home. Her ability to set the emotional tone and train the children will lend itself to bringing her husband good and not harm all the days of his life. (Prov. 31:12) This woman is no dowdy housewife, but dresses in attractive apparel. (Prov. 31:22) Her esteem is not low for lack of a vocation that brings her pleasure, but instead she is confident, clothed with strength and dignity, and can laugh at the days to come. (Prov. 31:25) She is capable, industrious, and a wise investor. (Prov. 31:14-18) She is

> **A virtuous woman will not settle for riff-raff when it comes to a man.**

constantly thinking of others and looking for ways to minister to the needy. (Prov. 31:20) Is it any wonder that her husband has full confidence in her (Prov. 31:11) and is respected at the city gate? (Prov. 31:23) What man wouldn't want a woman like this? She's a catch! This kind of woman does not settle for riff-raff when it comes to a man. The man she marries will be worthy of her virtuous attributes, for we are told he will arise and call her blessed and give her the praise she deserves. (Prov. 31:28)

Me submit to him? No way!

Well, if you thought we were going to get through a whole book on becoming a virtuous woman without discussing submission, you were wrong. The biblical concept of wives submitting themselves to their husbands (Eph. 5:22) has been given a bum rap by the world. Additionally, many Christians struggle with understanding the meaning of this scriptural principle. Webster's defines "submit" as, "to commit to the discretion or decision of another."

I like to think of it as "yielding." Remember, the Proverbs 31 woman was no doormat. She was out buying vineyards because she had earned her husband's trust. The concept of submission serves as part of God's plan to avoid confusion in the home. Let's face it, someone has to be in charge or it could result in anarchy. This is true for our country, the workplace, as well as many other groups where decisions are made. It is also true for the home. I dated some guys in college that, had I married them, it would have been a real struggle to submit to them. If I had been in the habit of virtuous dating, this alone would have served as a wake up call to end the relationship.

 The virtuous woman will succeed in being submissive to her husband's authority because she is first submissive to God. Trust me, submission to a godly man is hard enough. Now try to imagine the difficulty in submitting to a man who does not first submit himself to God's authority. Woe to the woman who does not take this into consideration before marrying! Submission is a command for wives and cannot be avoided in the pursuit to become a virtuous woman. I don't care how indoctrinated you are in the women's movement, I believe that deep within the heart of every woman is the need to be loved, cared for, and protected by a man. (Gen. 3:16) Who do you think is driving the market for romance novels and movies that highlight men coming to the rescue of the women they love?

As women, we all want to find our knight in shining armor, but it is critical that our knight be hand-picked by God and a part of the Lord's army. When it comes to dating, engagement, and marriage, the virtuous woman will not settle for less. Will you?

God's plan for some women may be to remain single. I have friends who have never married and are more content than some of my married friends with children. The virtuous woman does not stake her happiness on finding a man, but instead finds her joy in building her relationship with the Lord. Better is a single woman with a deep and growing relationship with Christ than a married one without such a relationship. For the woman who is called to be single, many opportunities abound to serve the Lord. God has not looked unfavorably on these women, but instead desires to stand in as the Groom. Many of these women have a faith that is to be envied, as they have taken full advantage of their opportunity to focus entirely on knowing Him and making Him known.

Whatever our call, whatever our purpose, as women we are all called to be virtuous. Unfortunately, few will ever reach that status. The virtuous woman is truly a rare find, yet I can imagine no greater pursuit. When all is said and done, I want others to remember me as a woman who feared the Lord, defined her worth in Jesus Christ, pursued godly wisdom, and found purpose in knowing God and making Him known. As a wife, I hope to be remembered by my husband as someone he could trust to bring him good all the days of his life. As a mother, I hope to be remembered by my children as a mom who looked well to the ways of her household, a mom who valued spending time with her children, and a mom who modeled the love of Jesus Christ and served Him with joy. In ministry, I hope to be remembered as someone who was faithful in sharing the Good News of Jesus Christ and its power to change lives.

"Give her the reward she has earned, and let her works bring her praise at the city gate" (Prov. 31:31).

But most of all, as a child of the living God, I hope to be remembered as fulfilling my God-given purpose to know Him and make Him known.

Encourage Your Group:
Actions for Group Study

1. In your opinion, what causes girls to enter into negative dating relationships?

2. Discuss your idea of a "godly date." Where do you go? What do you do? What do you talk about? How do you end the evening?

3. Discuss among your group the four types of dating that virtuous dating is NOT. Ask for testimonies from those willing to share.

The verse to support the CrossSeeker Covenant point of **purity** says, "Do you not know that your body is a temple of the Holy Spirit, who is in you, whom you have received from God? You are not your own; you were bought at a price. Therefore honor God with your body" (1 Cor. 6:19-20).

4. Discuss what it means when it says, "You are not your own."

5. Discuss reasonable standards for physical intimacy in a dating relationship (honoring God with your body).

6. Is it important to have this settled before you go on a date? Why or why not?

7. Discuss whether or not submission in marriage is essential in the pursuit to become a virtuous woman.

8. What five qualities would you like to be remembered for in your life?

Between You and God

1. Pray for a deep and personal relationship with Jesus Christ that can satisfy the longing in your heart to be loved and accepted.

2. Seek God's direction about your motives for dating.

3. Ask God to help you develop a plan as you accept a date, go on a date, and enter into a dating relationship.

4. Seek God's guidance on how you would rank the following in importance of dating, getting engaged to, or marrying a man who is … (Circle a number – 1 being "not important" and 5 being "extremely important.")

A believer	1 2 3 4 5
Submissive to God	1 2 3 4 5
A spiritual leader	1 2 3 4 5
A provider	1 2 3 4 5
A protector	1 2 3 4 5

5. Ask God to provide the guidance of a "Titus woman" in understanding what it means to submit to your husband. (Eph. 5:22)

6. When leaving a legacy, seek God's direction for how you are to be remembered by your:
   Friends
   Future husband
   Future children
   Your Lord and Savior

Commend those in your group study, your Titus woman, and Jesus Christ for providing you the guidance, wisdom, fear, instructions, and help this book has been able to give you. In your walk with Christ you are "the ideal woman" for this generation. I am honored you have spent this time with me through your study of this book. Carry on!

leader's guide

Leader's Guide

Virtuous Reality: Becoming the Ideal Woman is written to be a six-week study. The number of actual sessions will be dependent on you as a leader in guiding students through the various book sessions. The basic principles within the book are based on the CrossSeekers Covenant. The sessions seek to provide guidance on how each principle can be incorporated into their lives. Therefore, as you think about using the book as a CrossSeekers resource, all icons are applicable.

The book is interactive throughout. In each chapter you will find a number of tools you may use to teach the session. Some of these are:
- Sidebars
- Scripture references
- Questions and fill-in-the-blanks
- Stories which can be shared within a session
- "Encourage Your Group"
- "Between You and God"
- Highlighted text for specific use

As a group leader, we would encourage you during each session to:
- Be curious—Desire to be a godly woman and study His Word continuously.
- Be interested-Show the women in your group you are interested in them.

Tips for Godly Leadership
- Be constant—Lead each of the sessions by showing a caring spirit and by starting and ending on time. Remember, these are busy women.
- Be in contact—with God, with His work, with the young women in your group. If they have email and you have it as well, use it to communicate throughout the week.
- Be the "Titus Woman"—Many questions will arise among your group. Allow them to know that you are available to them at any time...and be a helper!
- Be watchful—Look for God at work among the women in your group. Allow them time to share with you and the others during each session.

- Be responsive—Answer God's call to make new insights a part of your own daily walk. You will find time to share these and encourage the others.
- Be positive—The temptations are real in the lives of these young women. Be an encourager who knows everyone in the group can succeed in becoming the ideal woman.
- Be un-preachy—We're sharing this word with you to remind you not to lecture. College women are lectured to everyday. Lead by sharing the insights you gain as you discover your own life as an adventure towards being the ideal woman.
- Choose six weeks or more that are convenient for the college woman.

Leading the Sessions: Seven Tips

1. Facilitate the discussion. Using the interactive points within each session, encourage each member of your covenant group to share.

2. Encourage each member to begin their study with prayer. Model for the students the process of inviting God into your sessions.

3. Introduce a "no-slam" rule. Insist that group members never put down another's comments, ideas, or concerns.

4. Be sensitive to the fact that this may be the first "covenant group" the students are involved with. Establish some ground rules with the members of your group. Some of these might be during each session:
   a. Respect the privacy of each person.
   b. Do not try to "fix" others.
   c. Do not interrupt someone else as she shares.
   d. Talk about as much as you listen.

5. Use open-ended questions to encourage talking and sharing. These require more than a yes-or-no or pat answer.

6. Lead the group in a discussion built around the questions in "Encourage Your Group" at the end of each session.

7. Close the group by prompting members to complete the "Between You and God" section privately.

 # CrossSeekers Resources

CrossSeekers: Discipleship Covenant for a New Generation
by Henry Blackaby and Richard Blackaby
Discover the six CrossSeekers principles brought to life in a user-friendly, practical, story-telling format. This study sets the stage for an exploration of each CrossSeekers Covenant point. Biblical and contemporary examples of promises made, promises kept, and promises broken, along with consequences, bring the biblical truths home to today's college students. ◆ 9 sessions ◆ Interactive in format ◆ Leader's helps included ◆ $8.95 ◆ ISBN 0-7673-9084-9

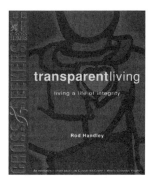

CrossSeekers: Transparent Living, Living a Life of Integrity *by Rod Handley*
Integrity. Everyone talks about it. God *delights* in it. We *demand* it. But what exactly *is* integrity, and is it important? If you want to be a person of integrity, to live the kind of life Christ modeled—to speak the truth in love, to stand firm in your convictions, to be honest and trustworthy, then *Transparent Living, Living a Life of Integrity* is for you! This study supports the CrossSeekers Covenant principle *integrity.* ◆ 6 sessions ◆ Leader's guide included ◆ $6.95 ◆ ISBN 0-7673-9296-5

CrossSeekers: The Challenge—Transforming the World Through Covenant Living *by David Edwards*
LifeWay offers your church lots of ways to reach students who are not only seeking to fully develop themselves academically, but develop a personal relationship with Christ as well. Written by popular collegiate speaker and teacher Dave Edwards, this resource is designed to take collegians through eight interactive sessions of moving deeper spiritually into covenant living as a CrossSeeker.
◆ 8 sessions ◆ $7.95 ◆ ISBN 0-7673-9295-7

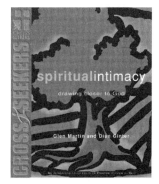

CrossSeekers: Spiritual Intimacy, Drawing Closer to God
by Glen Martin and Dian Ginter
Spiritual Intimacy will intensify the desire of your heart to know God more intimately, help you realize where you are in the process of drawing closer to God, and show you how to move ahead by knowing God on six successive levels. This study supports the CrossSeekers covenant point *spiritual growth.*
◆ 6 sessions ◆ Interactive in format ◆ Leader's guide included ◆ $6.95
◆ ISBN 0-7673-9427-5

CrossSeekers: Holy and Acceptable, Building a Pure Temple

by Dave Edwards

First Corinthians 6 tells us that our bodies are temples of the Holy Spirit. But what does that mean, and why should we care? This study looks at what it means for us to be God's temple. Through Bible study and contemporary situations, the physical, mental, and spiritual aspects are explored, along with their interrelatedness, as well as what to do when you fail in your pursuit of purity. This study supports the CrossSeekers Covenant principle *purity.*
♦ 6 sessions ♦ Interactive in format ♦ Leader's guide included ♦ $6.95
♦ ISBN 0-7673-9428-3

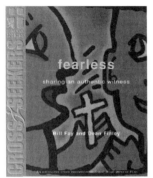

CrossSeekers: Fearless, Sharing an Authentic Witness

by William Fay and Dean Finley

Fearless, Sharing an Authentic Witness equips collegians for sharing their faith with others. Sessions address concepts such as our lives as a living witness (using the CrossSeekers Covenant points for discussion), how Jesus shared with persons He met, learning where God is at work in another person's life, a threat-free and effective method for presenting the gospel, and addressing difficult questions/situations. Based on *Share Jesus Without Fear,* this study supports the CrossSeekers Covenant principle *witness.* ♦ 6 sessions ♦ Interactive in format ♦ Leader's guide included ♦ $6.95 • ISBN 0-7673-9865-3

CrossSeekers: Virtuous Reality, Becoming the Ideal Woman

by Vicki Courtney

Virtuous Reality challenges college women to become ideal women as defined by God's standards, rather than the world's standards. The primary Bible passage that forms the foundation of the book is Proverbs 31, which describes a virtuous woman with worth far above rubies. Sessions of the book attempt to dispel the world's definition of the ideal woman. They address key qualities of a virtuous woman, and emphasize the importance of college women basing their worth solely on Christ. Sessions also challenge women to pursue wisdom, discern folly, develop a healthy perspective on dating, and discover their God-given purpose in life. ♦ 6 sessions ♦ Leader's guide included ♦ $6.95 ♦ ISBN 0-6330-0455-3

Transitions: Preparing for College

compiled by Art Herron

For high school juniors and seniors *and their parents.* Practical help for the transition from high school to college—the admissions process, financial aid, loans and scholarships, lifestyle changes, spiritual development, and more!
♦ 6 sessions ♦ Leader's helps included ♦ $7.95 ♦ ISBN 0-7673-9082-2

To order toll free, call 1-800-458-2772 or contact us at our website.

For more information, visit our Web site: **www.crossseekers.org.**